MW01489408

ZEROING OUT
The Secret to Peace
& Personal Power

ZEROING OUT
The Secret to Peace
& Personal Power

*A Guide to Regaining Your Peace
And Tranforming Peace into Power*

by
Bo Sebastian

Finding Authentic You Publishing
2024
Boca Raton, Florida

We enjoy hearing from readers. You can contact us from:
https://bosebastian.com
10 9 8 7 6 5 4 3 2
Cover Design: David Menton
Interior Design: David Menton

TABLE OF CONTENTS

INTRODUCTION:
Gray Matters

You are working overtime at your job, laptop open, sipping on strong coffee and eating donuts instead of dinner. Your laptop needs a charge, so you plug in the adaptor. However, your body and brain, which also need a recharge, keep working because of deadlines and a desperate need for the overtime pay.

You are running on net-zero energy, physically depleted and desperately needing a positive charge for your brain and body.

You have neglected your health for too long. All the signs are there. You've gained weight, you haven't gone to the gym in months, your diet is nonexistent, your fuse is short, and your energy shortage is now affecting the essential organs of your body.

In the coming chapters, I'm going to show you how to undo the negatives in your life and turn your body into sanctified ground, full of potential with a charge that will last the entire day.

Without a life change, your stress levels could begin to produce too much cortisol—the stress hormone. When the body is healthy, cortisol, the primary stress hormone, enhances brain function, tissue repair, and increases blood sugar when needed. However, when this natural stress response doesn't return to typical levels after an anxious incident, you will have a problem with low grade anxiety and stress.

This hormone can negatively affect many parts of your mind and body. Too much cortisol can lead to inflammation, a weakened immune system, elevated blood pressure, and high blood sugar levels, which ultimately results in Type 2 Diabetes.

Before I got up from my bed, I began making a mental list of what needs to be accomplished. I used my daily allotment of energy to appropriate free time between work, relationships, and chores. Without doubt, however, roadblocks and sidetracks littered my life with unexpected detours and drains of vital energy—often ending a tumultuous day with nothing left but shear exhaustion and no *me time*.

The *Zeroing-Out Technique* provides an easy-to-use method to recharge your brain by taking it completely offline for five minutes. The process is simple. Anyone can achieve it. All you need is willingness. Yet, most people say they can't get their minds quiet.

The meaning of meditation is: *to engage in mental exercise (such as concentration on one's breathing or repetition of a mantra) for the purpose of reaching a heightened level of spiritual awareness.* So, the secret to the meditative mind is to remove the obstruction of unwanted thoughts within the mortal mind. This will be our course of action in this text.

The best way to introduce this process is to use the metaphor of your brain acting like a computer. If you are working on your computer and all the windows of your desktop are open, it's hard to focus on the task at hand. However, when you close some of the open windows on the desktop you can focus more easily. The same thing is true with the *virtual desktop* of your computer brain. Just like your computer, you initially gain more memory and even more power by simply closing windows.

Each window on the desktop of your computer brain can represent stories you tell yourself from your past. If you don't close all of the windows or stories from your past, your positive charge in your body begins to deplete quickly. You find yourself drifting off in a dream when you're driving, while listening to coworkers, and it's hard to keep your mind on the present moment.

Can you produce good work when you're thinking of an argument you had with your companion? If what you yearn for is peace of mind, you must learn to shut down the negative stories in your brain. Doing so will help give you a positive charge and keep your brain acute. I call this *minimizing the stories* (or windows) in your computer brain. *Clearing its cache* is the mainframe of *the Zeroing-Out Technique.*

In the coming chapters, I am going to teach you to Zero-Out your brain. This five-minute process makes room for joy, self-care, potential, and a much-needed social or love life. I can show you how to get your anxiety level to near *Zen-Zero* with this simple exercise that can be accomplished in less than the time it takes to worry about it.

When you learn this simple exercise, you will immediately begin to feel the results of an energy renewal. Your mind can be keen and on-point even if your day is busy. You will have space in your brain to balance work with creativity, fun, and passion. You will consistently and easily regain the joy you once had.

The Stockbroker Who Invests in Energy

Thinking back on days of my own anxiety and stress, I had not given an equal share of my energy to things that mattered—like peace and security. In fact, peace shared the bottom of my daily to-do list with sleep and healthy food choices. (Well, let's just say that I always wanted peace, but I didn't desire it enough to change my bad habits.)

Chaos gained much of my brain's time and attention. If I were lucky, happiness became a bonus on good days.

A good stockbroker manages money by taking your portfolio and investing portions of it in stocks, bonds, gold, real estate, or mutual funds that will increase your net worth. When she makes good investments, you see an increase in your net worth. Bad investments, however, cause a depletion in available funds. If my energy had been money, I would have been knee-deep in the red. A person can truly want to increase his or her net worth, but never do anything that would increase savings and assets. This was me with my lack of energy.

Most people have an imbalance with the negative and positive investments of energy in life. Our relationship to the positive charge in life is not on equal footing with the negative discharge.

Fortunately, though, we each get 100% vital energy to utilize, every day, without fail. Each day, if we choose, we can begin to change how we invest our vital resources, specifically our outgoing energy.

Explaining why your physical and mental health

needs a shift will help you more understand the mechanics of Zeroing-Out.

The Human Computer-Brain

Continuing on with our computer metaphor, the human brain has a memory like a computer's hard drive. Once a moment in life happens, it is recorded in your human hard drive, becoming forever stored there. Every experience that you have ever had from the past is stored in your human brain in the form of words, emotions, or movielike memories. Given the right trigger, any thought from any part of your past is likely to haunt, intrigue, disturb, or delight you.

When you call up a memory from the past, it's like opening a file on the computer—you can:

- read it,
- edit it,
- observe it,
- attach something to it,
- transfer or send it to someone, or
- you can even throw it away, but this is far more difficult with imbedded memories.

Let's imagine, also, that when these past events are called to mind and opened on the virtual *hard drive of your brain*, you attach emotions to each memory. So, any subsequent time you recall this same memory, you may also experience this attached emotion along with the past incident you recalled.

Memory Recall + Emotion

You may use your computer brain to call up memories that help you achieve your goals or accomplish your work. For example, you may use your stored information to resolve technical problems, teach a class, sing in the shower a song you miraculously remembered from your childhood, recall the time when your baby was born, or even do surgery from the terabytes of information you have stored and studied in college. This is the positive side of calling up memories from the hard drive of your brain.

But compartmentalizing the good from the bad becomes the hardest human condition. Most people can't seem to call up good memories without also recalling some negative ones. We think about (click on) one positive file in our computer brains, but instead of one file opening, the entire folder pops open—rife with the hows, whys, maybe-nots, and wish-it-hadn't happeneds.

Sense Memory Recall

Actors take these same annoying memories from their own past to portray a character. They are masters at understanding the impact of how thinking about a single memory from the past while delivering their lines from the written script can positively or negatively color whatever they say. Great actors use these memories of actual incidents in their own lives as they speak the written script, allowing them to express emotions that parallel the storyline in screenplays and theater and bringing true life to the words.

In acting this is called using *subtext*. In Method Acting, an actress speaks a line, while she recalls an emotional event from her past. For example: the script may require an actress to speak the words, "I love you." The character, however, may hate her husband and be in love with someone else in the story.

She must show the audience this powerful twist of fate by how she delivers the line—not by the words in the dialogue, but by her emotions. She does this by allowing *subtext* to go through her mind while speaking the written line. She may imagine a time in her own life when she dated a man who abused her, then uses the subtext: *you will soon die, you asshole narcissist,* while she speaks the words, "I love you."

While subtext gives us insight into the depth of thoughts and history of the character, it also requires the actor to recall emotions from the past over and over again, especially in live theater, where they may have seven or eight shows a week. We see the actress pretends to love her husband while she plots to murder him. She does this all by recalling a horrible memory as she speaks her lines.

Watch carefully your favorite movies and television shows to search for times when actors say specific words but are thinking something completely different! Everyone can see the real power of the emotion in the eyes or hearts of a good actor—but not so specifically in the written words alone.

Truth being told, most of us—especially empathic people—*feel* what people *think* more than what they *say*. These internal words or subtext that we hear with our hearts usually hold a *mental equivalent* of a feeling that our lovers, friends, and coworkers want to convey, but are often afraid to communicate with just words. Basically, most of us feel energy and intent when someone speaks, rather than listening only to the words.

This acting technique makes lines and characterization personal to the actor. However, in real life, you do this all the time without even trying when you are reliving something negative in your mind while trying to do your work. You try to show compassion or love, while your sad thoughts taint and change the impact of your words to your children, coworkers, and spouse with negativity. Remember, people often can feel what it is inside your heart, even though you are counting each word and deliberately trying to say the right things.

This is the perfect metaphor of how someone's actions and intent cause us to feel strong emotion more than listening to their words. As you learn about the Zeroing-Out Technique, you'll realize that we cannot truly be authentic in word and deed, unless we stop reliving the past in our brains and focus in on the here and now. Your negative stories may be creating incongruent subtext with all the people in your life.

We *act* all day and don't realize how brilliant we are at the craft. We may have a perfectly normal conversation with someone, and not even realize how much our own subtext (those emotions that we think about) color our discourse and interactions.

Our Innate Ability to Act as If

Have you even noticed that your stress and anxiety is strongly affecting your close relationships? The people with whom you want to stay close have been distancing themselves from you.

Your brain is a complex, human mechanism. This same overloaded clutter in your brain can also cause you to be curt with someone and have a short fuse.

The human brain can be dynamic, with certainty. But when your brain is in sense-memory overload and you are over thinking about work, finances, family members, friends' struggles, you may end up letting your negative emotions trigger you with the people you care about the most. We are all prone to this.

Without realizing it, though, you are creating negative subtext in your conversations by fretting about work when you talk to your family, for instance. You aren't wanting to convey the negatives, in this case. Still, your friends, colleagues, and loved ones see the clutter and anxiety in your brain, even when you want to hide it. Remember, your loved ones emotionally hear your subtext rather than just the words you speak. They feel the stress, even though you don't speak it aloud.

Your conversations can become cluttered with emotions from the past, as well. For instance, you may have attached self-esteem and pride to a memory when you received a standing ovation after an inspired speech you gave in high school, for example.

A coworker, perhaps, describes a speech he gave at the office before you arrived that morning. Instead of intently listening, you begin to think about your own speech you once gave. After a few moments of remembering that one great event, your mind spirals into a deep tunnel of old memories. You remember something else that your computer brain attached to that old memory, a negative U-turn in your thought pathway leading to something sad.

In one moment, you are trying to give a friend your ultimate respect by listening to his story. In that same moment, your mind floats away into a negative memory. Suddenly, you are impacted by the goings on in your brain and not present at all for your coworker. This reveals signs of an anxious brain. Now you begin to attach something else to the recall:

Memory Recall + Emotion + Feelings =

Remembering Sadness

Again, this is a result of too much clutter in your brain buffer. Though you may want to stop the stories and focus, you simply don't know how to control your own thinking brain. The negative stories continue and your stress amplifies.

My Research into Anxiety and Stress

At the start of my research into the challenge of storing negative energy in our brains, I discovered that my own tricky brain even recalled happy memories to fool me. I got *smoke-screened* into following the steady trail of happy thoughts. Then suddenly, without provocation, my good memories turned into bad ones when that video in my brain led to a dead-end, perhaps, the death of a loving relationship.

No matter how hard I tried, my brain seemed to stay pigeon-holed on memories of the past that kept me asking the question *why. Why didn't I notice her more? Why didn't I see that his late nights at work were a ruse?* Or, if I were on a diet, something as benign as: *Why didn't I choose salad instead of pasta for dinner?* Why, why, why?

We want and need answers to the unsolved mysteries of the past. Unfortunately, there is no quality answer to the question *why*. The question *why* in your mind is a breeding ground for negative stories. If you stop asking the question *why*, you will have less clutter in your brain and ultimately be happier. I promise.

Memories That Keep You from the Now

From the moment you begin your walk down memory lane until you lay down your nostalgia for the night, you become *an absentee* in your present life.

To amplify this, if you are the slightest bit empathic or sensitive, you use the active part of your brain to recall issues from your past relationships, jobs, family problems, and form a negative polarization, rather than a positive one. You keep recalling melancholy memories, hoping to find the answer to the multitude of *why*s.

I'm also willing to guess that you spend the majority of your time driving, walking, and conversing with yourself—in your own mind—always thinking about something other than what is happening right in that moment.

Unfortunately, our present moment is gone the instant we live it. And... we have spent our lives mourning the past without regard for this gift of the now.

Happy or sad, you daydream a lot. It's hard to stay present. You lie awake most nights reminiscing about what *could have been* or wondering what the guy you're dating *really meant* in his last text.

If you are sensitive to people and their actions, I'm also willing to guess that you spend a great deal of time attracting or managing *energy vampires* (people who steal your energy with their negativity). And...

- In a world of chaos outside; in a world of chaos internally; where do you find your peace?
- Does peace even exist in the human brain?

I have good news for you, my friend. If you've stayed attentive up to this point, congratulations. I am ready to take you on a journey in the coming chapters *to Zero Out* your negative thinking, so you can take back your happiness and power.

Releasing the chaos in your brain makes space for dreams. Dreams reveal the depth of your passion and uncover a subconscious worldwide web of creative superpower that most of us have yet to discover.

When you make this exchange in your brain from chaos to potential, your subconscious mind becomes a reformatted hard drive ready to store and recall joy, peace, and anything else positive in your life.

Do you want this?

Do you *really* want this? Do you want your next moments more than you despair over what has passed by you? The essential keys lie ahead.

CHAPTER ONE:
What Is Anxiety?

To get rid of anxiety, you would first want to understand what it is. The following story exemplifies how anxiety could become a part of your life by holding on to lingering fears from the past.

You come home from work, get out of your SUV, and proceed to your front door with a bag of groceries from the butcher in your right hand and your briefcase in your left. You're halfway to the door when you see a ferocious Siberian tiger five hundred feet away, the same one that bit his handler, last night, and escaped from the city zoo.

Your heartrate instantly quickens as you move toward the safest escape from danger. Your fast response gets your keys directly in the door lock. You open and close the door without a hitch. Now you find yourself with your back leaning against the door and gasping for breath, hugging the bag of raw meat and dropping your briefcase. Your quick response kept you out of immediate danger.

The *sympathetic nervous system's* reaction of extra *adrenaline* and *cortisol* coursing through your veins, the fight or flight reaction, is great to keep you from eminent danger. But you don't live where wild animals or threats of this kind exist every day. You live in a city or nice suburban neighborhood.

On the other side of danger, you should begin to enter the relaxation mode, the *parasympathetic nervous system's* response to safety. Your body should be decreasing the flow of fight-or-flight cortisol and adrenaline, slowing down various nervous system functions, because danger is no longer present. You should begin to breathe more easily. Your heart should slow. Your stomach ease.

However, instead of relaxing, your brain feels muddled, your stomach sick, and your heart continues to thump. *What just happened?* you think.

You lock the door from the inside of the house to protect yourself from the tiger outside. Your irrationality now thinks that the tiger can turn the doorknob and get into the house.

Suddenly, you hear the tiger bounding against the front window. He growls ferociously. Your body and your brain still believe you are in severe danger.

You ask *Siri* or *Alexa* to call the ASPCA, as you move to another room farther from the front window and lock and bolt that door, as well. You whisper to the operator about your dangerous and precarious position. In your mind the tiger is getting smarter than a human. Your distance from the tiger doesn't provide enough space from danger. You nervously rush to the dank basement and lock yourself there until the ASPCA arrives.

For the first time during this emergency does your cognitive mind see what just occurred. It's as if you are playing a quick rerun of the chain of events in your mind, perplexed again by the questions *why* and *how?*

Even still, your brain and body recognize safety as you sit *presumably* secure in the dark basement, behind three locked doors, barricades, and a great distance from the ferocious tiger living rent free in your anxious mind. Your brain stops emitting fight, flight, and freeze chemicals into your body—for a moment.

Then, you begin to wonder if every latch was secure, every bolt fastened. *Why is help taking so long?* You even wonder if you had seen a mirage. Was the tiger simply the neighbor's German Shepherd?

Meanwhile, from the basement window, you notice the stealth tiger's body circling the house. *Definitely not the neighbor's dog!* You duck behind the air conditioning unit among the cobwebs, suspecting the threatful animal can see and smell your presence. You notice a long shadow of the tiger lingering in the descending sunlight. You sit in the dark cellar, on the cold cement of your brain's chaos, now trembling uncontrollably until help arrives.

You can't seem to calm yourself. Your brain still feels eminent danger, even though you've taken every precaution. Your sympathetic nervous system's responses to your stomach, heart, and brain keep you tense and nervous. You can't relax. You won't relax until you're sure the tiger is safely back at the zoo.

After the ASPCA affirms the tiger has been caught and secured, you recognize that you cannot release the generalized fear of *not being safe and secure in your own yard or home.*

As you watch the story on the local news that

evening, you recognize your front yard in the footage. You admire the two beautiful crepe myrtles you planted from twigs ten years ago. Between the pink flowering trees, a ferocious shot of the tiger. The news also flashes an old glamour photo of you as the person who stumbled upon the missing tiger. You're the town's hero. Yet, you wonder how this hero will ever feel safe in her own home again.

The Struggle Continues Long After

I had this same antagonizing, generalized fear after my home had been burgled and, similarly, after my car had been looted while on a fifteen-minute trip into the local Walmart. Anyone's brain can be triggered by similar *tigers* from the past—presenting equally dangerous ideations in the present moment. Even dreams can cause the exact fight, flight, or freeze reactions in your body as when you had met the original threat. This kind of low-grade anxiety can linger, sometimes, for years.

This tiger example is a clear explanation of how someone acquires *Generalized Anxiety Disorder* or GAD. The amount of fear your body holds onto *after* a dangerous event will also dictate the amount of fight, flight, or freeze chemicals emitted into the body to flee from any perception of danger in the future. Now, even the thought of a tiger or your neighbor's dog triggers that same fear memory.

This response (heart beating fast, brain muddled, even sweating) happens whether the danger is actual or imagined. Your body and human brain do not know the difference between what actually happened and what you imagine is happening now.

This means that in talk therapy, you can discover *what* you fear and *when* your fears began. However, those two years of talk therapy—alone—will barely change your neural pathways and the chemical and neurological responses to fear within your brain. Those old feelings and responses are now memories imbedded in your *amygdala*—the tiniest part of your brain that secretes these chemicals.

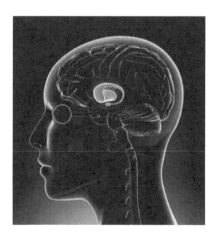

The reason why you can run so fast away from danger, lift something heavy off of a lost kitten, or brake your car so quickly when a swift bicyclist passes in front of your car is a result of the tiniest part of your brain, the amygdala, sending a message to react quickly with a deluge of fight or flight chemicals. Only after you have reacted, do you begin to understand what occurred in the cognitive part of your brain.

First, the amygdala reacts;
Then, we understand cognitively.

Think about the nervous system's process in this way: if you had had time to deliberate your response to danger, you would, in most cases, not react swiftly enough. You would have injured that biker who didn't stop at the traffic light and would still be wondering why you didn't react quickly enough.

The chemicals that the amygdala secretes are meant to create a swift, autonomic reaction in your body and to your limbs. The time to deliberate happens **after** you are safe from danger. At least, that's what I think the Creator had in mind when developing your brain.

If you experience GAD, somewhere in your past your amygdala had probably memorized a fear reaction that you can't seem to dismiss.

Now, you are faced with **unmemorizing** something that has become an automatic, autonomic response. You must get to the root of the fear and **release your reaction** to the fear with a process that clears out the anxiety *and* the response to that specific memory.

However, recalling the fear can trigger it, as you well know. Talk therapy hasn't been working fast enough.

You must use a retraining process of the brain's amygdala (the fight, flight, or freeze trigger); otherwise, anxiety will continue to plague you for the rest of your life. It will inhibit you from:

- safely going out of the house for fear of tigers behind every bush;
- riding an elevator because you once got stuck there for an hour;
- driving onto the interstate, because you were in a collision;
- being in a crowd, because you heard on the news that some people were crushed in a mass escape from a sold-out concert; or
- speaking in front of a large group of people, because you hiccupped when you were called on at work to give your point of view on a project.

Your unconscious fears are imbedded and sometimes even superimposed upon your consciousness. To gain access to these old memories, we need a pathway directly to the problem in the amygdala.

Though hypnosis alone may help your body on the pathway back to the calm of the *parasympathetic nervous system's* relaxation response, what about the memorized part that makes your heart thump, creates anger, shifts your mind to the past, and causes your stomach to ache?

Hypnosis is a fine first choice to unhook from the fearful response. But, without a retraining process of the tiny amygdala, you may imagine a tiger hiding behind every corner—long after the threat of danger. You might finally get to sleep and then dream about *"lions, and tigers, and bears."*

Perhaps, one of those hidden files of fear nested deep in the hard drive of your computer brain comes to the surface to frighten you while you dream. The roars are loud. They awaken you with a pounding heart. This scenario is certainly possible and highly probable, since we often process life in our dream state.

*Does your body know the difference
between reality and a dream?*

In fact, the brain often thinks the thoughts of a dream are even more real than reality. Who do you think is the creator of your dreams, if not *you* making every character speak, designing the scenery, recreating your high school lockers, being late for the next period's class, forgetting your lines in the school play, and misplacing your wallet at an important work dinner?

Think of waking up from a nightmare—shaking and cold. This is the amygdala's response to whatever your brain *perceived* was real while you slept. Your nervous system is trying to make sense or process your fears in your dreams.

This is most definitely why you wake up feeling your heart pounding and body sweating. This is often why anxious people can't sleep. Their brains subconsciously try to protect them from the hidden fears that might come up during sleep. They are afraid of something in the past:

- An abusive ex sleeping too close,
- An alcoholic mother or father spewing angry words, or
- An unfinished task looming.

In my twenties and early thirties, I wasn't sure what kept me awake at nights. I had a sense of generalized fear almost constantly. The reason I didn't understand that my mind was trying to make sense of my fears is because my dreams were creating *metaphors* of my fears, not realistic encores of them.

For example, my childhood experience with a mean father had become a monster chasing me in my dreams. My sexual abuser as a young boy appeared as a beautiful woman who turns into a two-toothed, bad-breath, psycho in the middle of sex.

The fear of death and of losing control were strong for most of my younger life; especially, before the age of thirty-five. How is it that I or anyone can get rid of these fear impulses that affected our lives in the past without our permission? This thought plagued me late into my thirties.

As a young man, anxiety exuded from me in all ways, including my love language. I was a posterchild for anxiety. My many bad relationships, however, helped me to discover some important facts about the brain. What became the most interesting fact was that there was a parallel with my anxiety and my insomnia.

I'm a hypnotist by trade. I help people get to a sleeplike state every workday. However, sleep eluded me most of my life. In fact, my sleep issues began my exploration into hypnosis.

Also, even though I have a brain, I didn't know its physiology. I didn't know a brain cortex from an amygdala, let alone what kinds of chemicals the brain discharges and physical responses they created in my own body.

I was like a Christian who had never read the bible yet tried to convert the world with limited knowledge of only one particular chapter or verse. I decided that it would benefit me and my practice to research science for the cause of my anxiety. I then discovered I had a fascination about the mechanics of the brain that is now unquenchable.

Not long before I became a hypnotist, in 1991, I had my first hypnosis sessions with a therapist who was a master hypnotist. I arrived at the front desk of her newly built condo near Central Park West in NYC.

I was told by her stern doorman to catch the elevator to the fifteenth floor and wait there. "The hypnotist will be with you when she's ready," he said robotically.

A long-haired, tiny, middle-aged woman with a strong Long Island accent made me *stand* outside her apartment door for almost thirty minutes waiting anxiously. When she finally let me in, it was clear she had been eating a leisurely lunch from the pungent, sulfur odor of egg salad and fresh-brewed coffee.

When I entered her lavish apartment, I already didn't trust her. In New York, a long wait was expected for the bank, post office, and every major retail store. But, for a private, $250 appointment with a hypnotherapist in 1990, not so much.

Ms. Hypnotist spoke with me for about thirty minutes before she asked me to relax on a very uncomfortable couch—not meant for reclining. She prepared me for what I'd now consider a haphazard hypnosis session. She led me through some breathing exercises, which is basic in hypnosis. When she thought I was relaxed, she began suggesting stress-free thoughts to my subconscious. She told me with complete assertiveness that I would no longer have trouble sleeping throughout the night.

To her credit the hypnotist recorded the session on a cassette tape, which may tell you how long ago this incident took place. When I got back to my own 500-square-foot NYC sublet apartment, I listened to the cassette about three times before I went to bed that night.

To my delight, I achieved a few years of moderately consistent sleep. I used the cassette she made me, most nights. After listening to the tape so many times, I began to memorize it. Subsequently, I taught myself how to self-hypnotize without even realizing it.

Maybe the anxiety from my past was still in my subconscious and kept me from sleeping, but now I had another, stronger message that edited the script in my brain: *Sleep is good! Sleep is for rest, not for processing fears.*

What I want you to understand about stress and anxiety is that there is *no easy fix* for the long-term problem of post traumatic stress and GAD (generalized anxiety disorder). Ongoing hypnosis and EMDR (Eye movement desensitization and reprocessing) sessions can help retrain the amygdala, with certainty.

But, on a day-to-day basis, on the road to complete recovery, we need tools that are less time consuming and more cognitively effective. This is why I developed Zeroing-Out.

You may need a complete overhaul of your anxiety buffer in your brain. But, as you move through that difficult process, you also need an easy fix for the temporary clutter in the brain buffer on a day-to-day basis.

Zeroing Out

CHAPTER TWO:
The Human Conundrum

Behind your closed eyelids, you have the opportunity to escape from what you see with your logical computer brain. When you close off the doorway to logic and the often-scary outside world, you begin the process of opening the potential of your creative mind or your dream state. This place beneath your closed eyes is where our journey begins—in the creative mind.

In your computer brain you often have an overloaded buffer of chaotic thoughts, playing like a screeching recording. So many messages, in fact, that some days, you can barely tell the real from the made-up, the authentic love from the masks.

Can you imagine a place, though, where peaceful potential grows, like a beautiful garden with every color, texture, and density of possibility?

If you can't imagine a peaceful place in your mind, then you must open your heart to the idea that peace is a real possibility. If you can't imagine the thing that you desire, the chances of better anything appearing in your life is slim to none. This is true with every one of your desires going forward. Visualize... Dream... Manifest!

Behind Your Closed Eyes

Start with this simple lesson. Close your eyes. What color do you see? Can you see color at all?

Sit with this process a little longer. Do you see just black and white, or can you see hints of colors, as well? Take a few minutes to sit quietly and notice what you see when you close off the outside world. When you do this, spend time observing what you notice, trying not to create words or mental lists in your brain.

Whatever you see, know that there is nothing wrong with your senses. You simply need practice with observing what is. Silence is a new language that you must learn to achieve to find peace. You are not going to be adept at anything with only one short lesson. With that in mind, just listen and observe the silence for a minute or two.

If you feel that you can't silence the machinations of your brain, you are correct. The brain's job is to provide reasoning. To get to peace you must ignore the brain by observing and listening. Listening and observing are diversion techniques to quiet the brain. Just be patient. You'll get there.

Now, try imagining a color? Use the color orange!

If you can't initially see the color orange, think about something more specific, such as the fruit. Imagine slicing into an orange and smelling the citrus zest. Imagine biting into a juicy wedge. Can you see it now? Or is it clearer in other senses—like taste or smell?

Some people think they must see an orange in their mind's eye to be competent at imagination. In fact, some individuals can imagine sounds better, some scents, some tastes, and yet others see more photographically.

Discover in this initial exercise:

- How does your mind imagine?
- Can you hear music in your mind?
- Can you imagine someone's touch?
- Can you remember a unique smell?
- Can you recreate the reaction of eating your favorite food?
- Is your imagination keen when it comes to sexuality and fantasy?

Note that if you spend a great deal of time in sexual fantasy, or thinking about food, or imagining a past conversation, or even hearing music in your mind; whichever way you fantasize, you will be more adept at those particular senses.

Let your senses lead you to those more distinct places for a couple minutes of silence. Then continue reading.

A Journey to Color

Between the age of twenty to almost fifty, I could see only glimpses of the rainbow of beauty and peace that existed on the canvas of my mind. The nonsense in my brain sounded more like a subway train almost constantly, always diverting my mind to chaos. I had no idea how colorful my life could be through the lens of a peaceful mind, because all I had ever heard were distracting noises.

A vast distinction exists between your brain's

memory and your mind's imagination. What you must understand is that your brain's *mental garbage* often blocks your view of the beauty that could exist in your life in the limitless world of the mind.

In my work as a hypnotherapist, clients often tell me this statement more often than any other after an initial session: "I have never felt more peaceful in all my life!"

I don't think I'm magical. I believe, however, that I took these individuals, using hypnosis, to a place that they had never visited before. I took them beyond the veil of their brain's clutter. This is where you, also, belong... for at least some of the day or evening.

Sensitive Minds (Sensory Defensive People)

Are you a person who can be 95% comfortable in bed, but one wrinkle in the sheets could keep you awake until you straightened and pressed out the wrinkle? Do you often find things wrong with your food at a restaurant? Do you have to wear a mask at department stores because of the perfumes? Can you feel negative people when they walk into a room?

You may be an empath, which initially makes life too loud, too strong, too crowded, too bright, and too much of just about everything. You may intensely feel the energy of everything and everyone around you.

If you are empathic, crowds, loud noises, needy people, and chaos can physically exhaust you. Powerful perfumes can give you migraines. You may avoid certain textures of food. When empathic people feel too much, this mental fragileness is known as *sensory defensiveness*. In other words, your senses think they must fight to defend you from being overloaded with too much of any sense. When your body detects a fight to protect itself, this tires you and causes fight or flight responses in your brain and body.

I am the poster boy of sensory defensiveness. As a result, I have been living on the fringe of my anxiety garden for a long time. An empathic life can be lonely, at first. Mine was. I assumed that I was different than everyone else in my life. Sensory Defensive people often get called "too sensitive," which makes us isolate.

As I have matured, I realized that different wasn't so bad. I am unique, with certainty. My overactive senses have led me to be a good musician—to be able to hear pitch; they have caused me to be a great cook, understanding the nuance of seasoning; also, they have encouraged me to help others, because I can often sense what others feel.

I am a *super-feeler*. Everything from my food to my entertainment to relationships deserve a long conversation with self. As a result, one of my fascinations about observing the machinations of my own human thinking is listening to the stories in my human brain. This, of course, requires getting quiet.

If you wait long enough, your brain will begin to connect tangents of thought. For example: You're sitting on a chair with no stimuli. Yet, you hear your own stomach gurgling. This leads you to wonder what you ate or didn't eat. The conversation in your brain begins. You imagine having dinner with an old friend when your stomach became upset from eating raw oysters. That same friend's father died recently. Then, you think about your own parents and wonder how long they will live, resulting in thoughts about how ephemeral your own life is.

Your brain is a genius at keeping your attention on stories and scenarios that have nothing to do with your peace, your joy, or your contentment. The habit of thinking in tangents is actually something you can shut off. Zeroing-Out will help this issue, as well.

If when you get quiet, you begin to think about a story that you tell yourself often; instead of shutting down the story, simply listen. Listening to your own brain without interruption is harder than it sounds.

Every night before bed, I sit on my recliner and clear my mind of the day and of my stories before I go to bed. If I try to sleep with all the clutter, I'll be awake all night.

Sleep cannot happen when you think deductive thoughts or listen to words in your brain. You can, however, sleep if you change the words to images. Pictures cause the mind to dream.

You must begin to control your thinking at some point, otherwise, you will be at the mercy of your past thoughts for the rest of your life. Listening to yourself or anyone requires a quiet mind.

One of the easiest ways to avoid chatter in the brain is to imagine the silence just after you ask a question.

What Your Brain Knows

Your brain doesn't really know facts unless you believe them. For instance, how does your brain know how old you are or why it matters—until your birthday arrives. The date comes, you get invited to dinner with friends, and suddenly you are older. Have you noticed that you feel older after your birthday? When you feel older long enough, you may begin to look older.

What if you decided that your friends, family, and the calendar couldn't tell you that you are one year older? They don't get to boast that they are younger than you, or older and wiser.

I gest about this aging idea, but I deliberate this truth often. What if you didn't tell yourself your age—or, for that matter, your problems? Your brain would have no rationale for keeping you stuck or frustrated. In other words, no chaos or anxiety would gather in the cache of your brain buffer to require aging, stress, or physical atrophy.

Yes, memories, like videos, are recorded and stored in your brain. But you don't necessarily have to play them continuously. Things could go through your brain but not stay there long enough to cause attrition. A birthday, each year, would go by without storing the fact that you *should* get one year closer to death. Instead, you'd live on an endless continuum of timelessness.

Is it possible? Ageless in mind, ageless in body. What color do you see in your mind now?

If you could keep other information from your brain's incessant recapitulations, maybe, your brain would tell you something other than that your relationship sucks, or that your job is stressful, retirement isn't what you thought it would be, or that your life is chaos-filled with no joy and love. Maybe you could simply live your life, dealing with it one moment at a time with no expectations.

Most of us tend to believe our documented stories of the past. We think we are listening to a true story being told to us by an intelligence worthy of our listening. But who is pushing and pulling the levers of your brain and telling you these grim stories?

These tales of the age are being told *by you—to you*—using an amazing computer memory chip forever lodged in your human brain that can retain and record everything you have ever done and spoken. To review all of the old videos of your past is just not something you want to stay up all night watching, deliberating, and reliving. Not now, not ever!

Aren't you ready to move on to your greatest potential, no matter your age or circumstance? Constantly meddling in your own past is not helping you get on with your best future.

Staying Away from Race Consciousness

Race consciousness also contributes to the clutter in your brain. Race consciousness is a common belief among most humans that seeps into your brain from television, movies, friends' and relatives' point of view, and from the Internet.

How do you sort through all the nonsense in your brain and get to the essential thoughts that propel you to your true potential?

The recorded video in your brain is like the wizard in the story of Oz. Not only is the wizard pulling the levers to distract you, but he seems to be feeding you malevolent information from the past and from race consciousness that makes you think too hard, stresses you out, and gives you the kind of anxiety that exhausts you. He makes you fragile like the scarecrow, inhibits you from feeling like the tinman, and creates fear as in the lion. You cannot even walk on your personal yellow brick road toward joy most days, because of your wily brain's clutter.

However, what happens in *The Wizard of Oz* when Toto (exemplifying truth) pulls back the red curtain to find that the wizard is just an old man (the past), who thinks he has the power to pull the levers of your computer brain?

When the curtain gets pulled back to reveal the old man, the wizard tries even harder to convince you that a tiny old illusion of a man isn't the wizard at all. "Look away!" he shouts.

Most people's first reaction to the demand: "Look away!" is to face in the direction where the past points. We look wherever we are told to look or told not to look.

Like our fascination with horror, we look where the bloody messes are, too. As a society, we barely ever observe ourselves long enough—our actions, our annoying thoughts—then ask the poignant questions that would solve the age-old mystery of who is pulling your anxiety levers.

You have allowed your own brain and the history of your past to point you to something other than the truth, something other than your moral compass and emotional authenticity. You believe that the answer to the formidable question *why* is somehow hidden in your past. You'll never find your answers in the mountains of old videos from the past.

The old man acting as the mighty wizard (the past) is *playing* God with you all day, every day. The wizard's demands are most definitely the reason for the chaos in your brain. Your personal computer chip is willing to use its information to keep you on its chaotic platform—like social media—so that you will systematically avoid life, joy, and peace.

That's the media's job, too. It also wants to tell you who to be, what is interesting, and where to keep your attention.

At night, while you should be sleeping, resting, and restoring your amazing human body and brain—while you should be charging your finite amount of energy—you, instead, want to engage with the skeptical, doubtful, and insecure stories from your past. Even more remotely we think about the nonsensical—the cast of characters from television, social media, and the news.

You are so afraid of the silence in your own mind that you fill your brain with just about anything on television, because it keeps your attention long enough for you to get tired and fall asleep. Tomorrow you'll find another way to fill the day and your brain with more junk. Can life really be this insipid?

What becomes even more intriguing is that this chaotic, computer brain chip of yours also has a portion of it that is completely designed to lead you *out of your chaos*. But... who wants to be at peace? Who wants to hear silence before sleep? Who would like to meditate for an hour? Maybe gurus and yogis? Certainly not a normal person like you or I, with sense and reason.

You have given the creative part of your brain no blank space to write a new or positive story. In fact, with your busy children, the massive number of activities on your daily schedules, your crazy work, your personal habits, your online activities, your whatever... you leave no space for space, empty space, or nothingness. In fact, Zeroing-Out scares the hell out of you. With nothing in your brain, what would you do or think about? Empty space feels frightening and insecure.

After you have done everything for everyone in your tiny world, listened to your own bullshit a thousand times, fought with yourself, worked eight or more hours bringing home the bacon, dealt with family problems, and spent your last nerve on that needy friend who sucks out your last bit of empathy, where is *your* personal empty space to recharge?

Without empty space there is no chance to recharge. You would not forget to recharge your cellphone, which only lasts about a day. How long will the charge in your brain and body last without shutting down completely?

CHAPTER THREE:
Inductive or Deductive Thinking?

For many years, I witnessed the difference between the average person who falls into a hypnotic trance easily and the highly sensitive or anxious person who barely ever stops thinking, struggling to let go. Simple relaxation exercises don't really help for the latter. This kind of client fidgets, scratches herself on the nose, coughs, and twitches, while I'm creating a very relaxing atmosphere. It's as if her body doesn't know how to relax.

I discovered the contributing factors that pushed all the wrong buttons in the physical bodies of my difficult clients to prevent a restful, great hypnosis session. This information was simple to observe as the practitioner.

What I didn't realize, though, until my own sleep problems recurred was that I was learning from my difficult clients why *I* couldn't get a restful night of sleep. Also, I began to understand why I had gradually become more anxious and stressed out during the time when the insomnia recurred.

My own, anxious amygdala started manifesting familiar patterns from my past that became harder to control. The thoughts and feelings were pressurizing inside my heart and body, leaving me wanting to explode. This left me with the question after twenty years of therapy: What hadn't I processed from my past?

PTSD Triggers

I remember, once, while I was out with friends for dinner and a movie, I sat comfortably in my theater seat waiting for a movie to start, a bucket of buttery popcorn between my legs, a bottle of water in the cupholder, and surrounded by love. I never once thought that, in that moment, something so real would happen on the movie screen.

Because of one poignant and scary scene in the movie, I found myself walking out of the movie theater, and an hour later, driving in the opposite direction of my home—mind muddled, heart pounding, and still holding fast to a bucket of popcorn. *What had just happened to cause this post traumatic event to occur?*

The movie's first scene from *Silver Linings Playbook* was an exact replica of a childhood drama. Robert Dinero even resembled my Italian father and sounded like his ferocious roar, as he beat up his teenage son, which in my mind was my own brother in the bunkbed below me.

From the beginning of the movie, it set the scene in my mind to relive a dangerous moment in my childhood. As it happened, I had lost control of my own body and mind. I remember telling my friends that I felt sick and needed to leave.

Later, in my car, I called my best friend, Keith, who happened to be a compassionate therapist. He *talked me down* from my precariously anxious ledge by making me count backward, subtracting 3 from 200, and so forth.

As I counted, he spoke calming and loving words about self-safety. He was there for me as my muddled mind recognized that I was *not* actually in that horrible moment of my past. When I returned to reality, I had driven an hour in the wrong direction from my house in Nashville, toward a distant farmland in south Tennessee.

Lessons Learned

In that moment, I realized I was dealing with a deep wound from my past that needed my attention. If I didn't heal the wound and retrain my amygdala, I would never be able to sleep peacefully. But, I didn't have the tools to help. How can you heal something that is buried in your subconscious?

I was back to the drawing board, trying to develop better tools for situations like this, which could happen to my clients and me at any time of the day or night. After a meditation one morning, I developed a process that freed my brain of my recorded loops of the past, which I now call *Zeroing-Out*.

With divine leading, I recognized that changing a habit, working on PTSD, and ameliorating fearful thoughts were all similar to the learned process of relaxation that I was witnessing with my anxious clients.

More exploration about the nervous system helped me realize that these anxious, memorized patterns of the amygdala also have the ability to reshape and create a metamorphosis toward healthy brain responses, as well. This is because of the neuroplasticity of the human brain, specifically the amygdala, which is the culprit for memorizing amygdala-based anxiety or PTSD in our computer brain. What I had not looked at was how the amygdala can also learn positive behaviors, too.

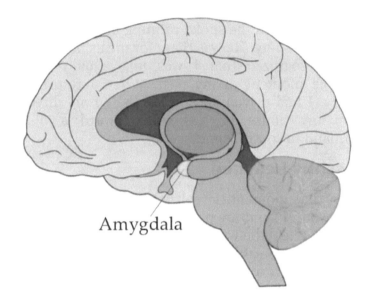

Amygdala

Developing Zeroing-Out

It was easy for me to become passionate about understanding the underpinning of Zeroing-Out, because I embodied many of the symptoms of my clients when they fidgeted during the walk down process of the hypnosis session.

I had lots of anxiety and PTSD from a childhood, rife with bad memories, which may come up later in the book if I need references. You can also get a handle on most of my old stories from many of my past books, specifically: *The Anxious Attachment of a Gay Man: Lessons Learned from Sex, God, and Life* found in any online bookstores.

Even in my novels, each fictional character replicates a reflection of my soul—but, perhaps, on steroids. As I was writing each book, my mind was looking for ways to gather the old characters who had hurt and abused me and recreate scenarios where the antagonist loses, dies, or gets destroyed in the same mayhem he or she built. Unfortunately, after years of writing books, the memories still lingered, much like realizing that years of talk therapy unearthed your pain but did little to release it.

I could write, rewrite, and edit my books, but I didn't have the same success with the stories in my own subconscious.

Solving my mental and physical challenges kept me always on the pathway to understanding the problems of my clients. My clients taught me my life's lessons, repeatedly, throughout the over thirty years of my practice. At one point, I gave up writing fiction and began to document real life. How grateful I am for that. My mind moved from bad dreams to dealing with my awakened, authentic reality.

Awake in the Brain

Even if you dream of a PTSD trigger, your amygdala doesn't know the difference between an actual threat and a contrived one, made up by your own subconscious in a nightmare. My unresolved issues had left me awake for many nights before my revelatory meditation began to create answers to my problem and for many suffering from PTSD.

My anxiety issues caused sleepless nights or secondary insomnia. The conditions below are a collection of my clients' and my own secondary insomnia issues:

- I feel as if I'm awake all night, agitated and restless;

- I fall asleep, then wake up panicky and energetic;
- Just as I get restful, I get a surge of energy, especially around my heart; sometimes this happens in my feet and legs, as well;
- My mind thinks all the time, even at night, while I'm supposed to be sleeping;
- I get overly sensitive, just as I begin to relax;
- I'm afraid to relax, because I'm ultimately afraid of death;
- I recall the past videos of my life, trying to recreate them with new endings, rewriting the old endings;
- Sleep reminds me of being sick or hospital sedation; and
- I have difficulty letting go of any- and everything from the past.

All the reasons above will not only prevent you from relaxation, they will also keep you anxious and stressed for the rest of your life. The primary reason—even though all the reasons above are valid—is because you cannot shut off your chaotic computer brain—awake or asleep.

When you clear the brain of deductive thought—Zero Out—you begin to clear a pathway to the mind, where peace and rest begin. Your imagination is the seat of your mind. It's where restful dreams are created.

All of your imagination is dictated by images, not spoken words in your brain. On the other hand, your brain is the seat of deductive reasoning, already conceived ideas and thoughts. So, one very clear way to see if your brain is deliberating in your deductive brain is to see if you are listening to a spoken voice in your head.

Peace doesn't happen in your brain like a voice

talking to you. The peaceful mind speaks in silence with beautiful images and dreams.

Eye-Popping Symbiosis

Your eyes and brain have a symbiotic relationship.

- The movement of your eyeballs directly relates to the activity of your human brain;
- When the eyeballs move to the right, you use your right brain;
- When your eyeballs move to the left, you use your left brain; and
- With your eyes open, if you stare at one place for one long, silent moment, you will notice that your mind slows down. I call this, simply—a *blank stare.*

When a hypnotist asks you to gaze at a light or a spot on the ceiling, while you breathe slowly, he or she is basically decreasing your brain movement, which starts the process of the parasympathetic nervous system relaxation.

1 + 1 Deduction = INSOMNIA

There are two major parts of the thinking brain. *Deductive thinking* is the awakened and active state of the brain. If you can add 1 + 1, you are using deduction. If you can answer any kind of factual question in your brain, decide something, or focus on a bad or uncomfortable problem from your past, you are utilizing the deductive, active, awakened, and rational thinking side of the brain.

Remember: if you think about something *deductively, you will never find peace or get to sleep.*

The internal part of the top of your head that some

call the gray matter, the part that thinks deductively, I'll refer to simply as the human *computer brain*. This term implies that your human responses to the movement and shifts in the brain's physiology are cause and effect.

Every human being has this hard-drive, human brain that holds autonomic brain responses and memories from the past. The automatic video recorder is always on and always documenting every moment of your life.

We also have a software-like part of the brain that accesses and utilizes the aspects that require task-orientation and learned behavior.

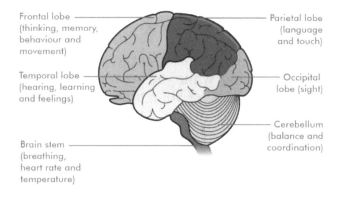

[https://socratic.org/questions/how-many-parts-is-the-human-brain-divided-into-is-one-of-the-parts-the-hind-brain]

You may have heard the term *monkey mind*. This term would suggest that you cannot control the body or brain with the lobes of the physical brain. However, you use your brain all the time to control parts of your body, to do functional deduction such as arithmetic, and to schedule important events. Surgeons use memory recall to access important physiological information during a complicated operation. The brain is not a monkey. *It's more like a computer with a video recorder, calendar, and hard drive.* To review from the first chapter:

- The brain creates a file—a new memory;
- We can open that file and observe it;
- We can edit that memory;
- We can add an emotion to that memory; and
- We can also throw the file into the garbage can.

These are all deductive choices.

We can also lose a file and forget where we stored it. Then we must use our computer brain's search mechanism, the big magnifying glass in the top right hand corner of your brain's computer screen. This is the frontal lobe of the brain.

Sometimes, though, like that magnifying glass which forages through every file on your computer, remembering just one person's first name—who is standing right in front of you—someone whose name you should absolutely have remembered is impossible.

In those anxious moments, I see fragments of what I should know, but not the entire memory. Perhaps, I begin to stutter the first syllable of the person's name out loud, trying to jog my memory. "No, that's not right... Is it?"

This is the *tip-of-the-tongue syndrome,* which is always filled with anticipatory anxiety.

Forgetfulness amplifies as we get older. Remembering someone's name or something intricate from the past becomes even more dumbfounding as the years pass. Is it because:

> *The older we get the more memories we must sort through to get to the answers?*

Remembering Mayhem

We have no trouble remembering our trouble with meticulous detail. Even so, I'm encouraged when I remember a song lyric from my childhood. Mind boggling. *Is this the same human brain that can't remember the name of my best friend's husband,* I ask myself?

Can you learn to relax while you are remembering something, and let the search mechanism of your brain complete its task? Truth be told, the more you fear NOT remembering, the worse the problem becomes. Or do you get frustrated and quit trying to remember and ask for help?

I can't tell you how many times I have told my husband that when I forget someone's name, *please, please, please... just put out your hand and introduce yourself! Ask the person his or her name...* to help your husband's slow-moving recall to remember this good friend's name!

So, with the deductive mind, we could also get caught in the problem of NOT remembering something, like a name. What you need to understand about this issue is that fear is the main culprit of not remembering something. As soon as fear enters the brain, mind muddling starts. Then, remembering a fact or a name is virtually impossible.

You'll notice that when you decide to stop thinking about whatever you are trying to remember, then all of a sudden, the memory clearly appears to you, as if you knew it all the time. And... you actually did.

The deductive brain is an intricate storage compartment for everything that you have done and experienced in the past. Like an old computer—one that has crashed for the last time—the anxiety stored in your brain will die along with your physical body. What's in the brain is like what's in your bank or your stock trading account after you die.

So, what extraneous brain data is so worthy of your worry that you keep all the windows open on your brain's desktop?

What value are chaotic facts kept so close, locked in a secure vault in your brain?

The lessons learned from your past are very much worth carrying with you into another lifetime or into the future of your spirit, whatever you choose to believe. Even if you're an atheist, how you dealt with your lessons becomes your legacy and memory.

At a time when cloud memory was not available and even hard drives looked like floppy disks, I owned an old laptop, which had a tiny hard drive that contained all my important, essential documents. I let my nine-year-old nephew play a video game on my computer, which he downloaded from the web without my permission.

From that one dark hour of my past, I never got to see any of my essential computer files again. They disappeared into the ether from *whence they came*, as did my first version, mint-condition, Apple laptop's hard drive.

With the dawn of cloud storage, I no longer have PTSD about that over-zealous nephew's accident. I wish there were, however, a cloud for the rest of the PTSD moments in my life. I would love to store a few of those rife-with-fear and filled-with-painful moments somewhere other than my computer brain.

Fortunately, for you and me there is a solution lingering just beyond the brain.

If you cannot relax without a pill or if you have generalized anxiety, then you need to know how to control the content of your human brain and when to drag its contents to the trash.

If you don't, you will hide many of the issues you don't want to face in metaphoric folders on the brain's hard drive. Like a computer's desktop—you hide the problems in a folder, within another folder, within another folder, within another tiny, misnamed folder like Russian nesting dolls.

Avoidant Behavior

Purposely hiding a memory like those old computer files is *avoidant* behavior. I sometimes call it *smoke-screen* behavior, like a smoker who goes for a cigarette to create a literal smoke barrier between the problems in the world and him- or herself.

When you successfully hide a feeling, your problems never come to the light to be examined, dealt with, and ameliorated. You can hide behind work, doing for children, computer games, necessary appointments, anger causing moments, frustration, social dealings, housework, problems in your relationship, and needy friends in life that are more important than your own mental health.

You can't control most things in life, especially other humans. However, you can learn how to control your own human brain—your own living, breathing, moving, functioning database inside your head.

You must first stop avoiding the problem. If you can see it, feel it, or taste it, the problem is there. If you want to get rid of a problem and throw it in the trash, you must first decide to learn a new way of dealing with it.

Getting angry at someone or frustrated with yourself hasn't worked in the past to stop your problem. Sleeping, if you can get to sleep, doesn't work. Working late into the night... not so much help. Smoking an endless chain of cigarettes while sipping scotch... nope. You need to learn a new system of decompressing the very real problems that exist in your human brain.

Learning something new and amazing, always takes time and practice, though. When you control the computer brain, you control fear-based and anxiety-related issues. You need to cut off the problem at its roots. Better yet, dig up the roots along with the problem, once and for all.

Even in 2024, there are many people—mostly older and not so much wiser—who won't even take the time to learn how to use a computer or a smart phone. In time, these same folks will be unable to function in a world that requires us to be computer literate.

You can train your brain. Most importantly, you can train the person—you—who listens and controls your brain. Being a proud owner of your brain, having read the manual, and knowing all its operating functions is going to be your primary goal in this book.

The Inductive Brain

The deductive mind operates primarily with fact. However, the inductive mind uses reasoning and relational framing—a human's ability to relate one thing to another.

If 1 + 1 = 2, then 2 + 2 = 4.

This inductive part of your brain, sometimes, leads to your dream state by means of logic, rather than relaxation. However, as explained later in this book, there are other, easier ways to get to peace and personal power; specifically by hypnosis (for lasting change) and, even easier still, by Zeroing Out (for change in a moment of stress or anxiety).

Try This!

With your eyelids closed, peer outward into the

darkness, beneath your eyelids as if you're staring out through your forehead.

Initially, when you close your eyes, you *should* see with your mind, not your brain. This is the perfect premise to begin.

A Caveat: I agree that the above statement is not 100% true, because many people daydream with their eyes open, and conversely, people can see into the past with their eyes closed. Initially, however, if we don't over think it, this test does help to understand the conceptual difference between the computer brain and the mind.

With your eyes open, your brain records what you see in the tangible world. Eyes closed, you primarily see with the mind, which holds infinity by nature. The mind is as large and as potent as you can imagine. Nothing limits the mind but the limited ideas of your human brain. What the mind holds is infinite possibility, if you are not limited to human facts, or what you inductively conceive from those facts.

What I don't want you to do in this exercise above is to close your eyes and see into a memory of your last moments with your eyes open, or any other memory, for that matter. Think about creating a dream world beneath your eyelids.

When we live in the recorded or stored part of our computer brains, we can't and won't ever get to the pathway toward the infinite. It is contingent upon this experiment to stay out of all memories to completely get to our creative abilities, relax, or get one iota beyond our anxiety and fear.

The Correct Eye Position

Imagine that you are sitting on a recliner in the most comfortable place you know. To use your mind, not your brain, you will need to imagine trying to look out of an imaginary window above and behind you. With your eyes still open and your eyeballs averted upward, begin to imagine an ocean view through the window above you and behind you.

Wait and stare a little longer at the beauty in your mind before you begin to let your eyes slowly close. See the majestic morning sky, as the sun rises. See white sea birds waking from their roosts and flying down to the sand to feed or to bathe.

See the sun, the color of an egg yolk floating on the deep blue ocean, creating a beautiful and sparkling reflection leading toward you. Gently let your eyes close as your imagination takes over. You will no longer need the vision from your physical eyes as your creative mind takes over your limited deductive brain. (I purposely didn't give you a photo of this, because I need you to use your imagination.)

This is the way you should softly close your eyelids to relax—almost as if reluctantly. When you close your eyes correctly and softly, you will still see a bit of light. Your eyelids may even quiver. This is perfect.

This quivering movement is exactly what your eyes do when they are completely relaxed, and you are on the verge of sleep. This entire process is basically creating a scenario where you feign sleep and dream.

Dog Lessons

I began to understand this phenomenon even more clearly from watching my puppy Coco fall asleep. He stares into space, then gently, without him even wanting to, his eyelids reluctantly close. I sense him feeling secure and comfortable as he lets out that last sigh, before he almost smiles and lets sleep envelope him.

Eyelids Locked and Loaded

The next objective is to get your eyelids to feel as if they are unable to open at all. Even when you try, they should feel as if something gently keeps you from opening them completely. However, you should wait about three minutes after your eyelids close to try this.

Make certain that you continue to stare upward, imagining something clearly in your mind like the ocean scene. This action gives the eyes a chance to retreat to a resting position.

You can imagine the face of a loved one or something as simple as a butterfly. If you have trouble visualizing things, you can also imagine listening to your favorite song before you *gently* try to open your eyelids. Hum along with the song in your mind. The more you imagine anything, you'll feel the muscles directly behind your eyes relaxing. This process simulates sleep and tells the body to prepare for *a dream state.*

Another method that works just as well is to close your eyes gently. Then imagine staring at the ceiling as if through a window that is above and behind you. This also causes a resting position in the eyes to occur. Imagine, while staring out of the window in your imagination, that you see a butterfly on the windowsill. Try to imagine the colors of the butterfly's wings. Remember that your goal is to keep your mind focused on what you imagine for at least three minutes.

After which, your *eyelids should feel stuck and closed*, which is the catalytic response to this resting positioning of the eyeballs. For me, the process above is a litmus test to see if I'm ready to enter a resting state.

When I discovered this trick, I realized that I had spent the majority of my life trying to sleep with my eyeballs pointing downward instead of upward, when my eyes were closed. Also, my eyelids were usually closed very tightly. Personally and with many of my anxious clients, we have to make a concerted effort to avert our eyes upwards and barely close our eyes to prepare the way for a peaceful mind.

This is, and continues to be, the biggest problem when it comes to the brain resisting letting go completely. With the eyes facing downward or straight forward, you will stay in the deductive mind all night. You may sleep, but it feels as if you're up all night thinking. Even after many nights preparing for sleep, I still have to do this exercise. My eyeballs desire to rest downward and forward. So, with this simple trick, I now sleep quickly and soundly.

As a test, try to open your eyelids to see if your eyeballs are in the correct place. If they easily open, then your eyeballs are in a downward or straight forward position. This is incorrect. These two latter positions help your brain to easily access the chaos in your stored files.

This mistake in the positioning of your eyes will prevent you from resting, dreaming, and keep you from getting to a meditative state, every time. Checking to see if your eyelids are locked is an easy thing to do right after you get into bed or before a meditation or nap.

For the eyelids to lock closed, the eyes must be averted upward, or they must be staring as if you see a spot on the ceiling.

Silence is Golden

Ultimately, to achieve *Zeroing-Out*, the deductive part of the human brain must rest.

- No chatter.
- No wondering what's on the grocery list.
- No thinking about how often you're going to have to urinate tonight, because you drank too much water before bedtime.
- No more conversing with yourself—at all.
- Even your eyeballs must submit to rest.

You wonder why you can't stop the brain from feeding you information all the time, yet you keep the laptop of your brain open 24/7. You don't put your computer brain to sleep, as you would your own personal computers. Even your computers need to rest. Even your electrical devices need to be recharged. With rest comes renewal and a recharging for the computer.

Nothing is going to change on that hard drive between the time you shut off the computer brain and when you wake it up again. Remind yourself of this self-imposed demand many times all day, all week.

If this doesn't work, try the method explained below:

Imagine that you are casually walking through a beautiful Japanese garden. You arrive at a wooden bridge that arches gently above a small creek filled with huge koi. You move to the center of the bridge on the arch and look downward toward the clear water.

You notice that the fish begin to surface. Alas, they swim around you with their mouths gaping. *Feed me!* they seemingly say. You are delighted.

Look at all the different colors and kinds! They want me. They need me to feed them. I must. Yes, I must feed them.

You have some food in your pocket, so you throw a handful of fish food into the water. The koi jump and fight over the food. Then, they stay there beneath you, waiting to be fed again.

They might as well be saying, Where's my damn food? I thought you wanted us. Didn't you beg for us to be beneath you and pay attention to you? You did. We heard you. Feed us again!

In fact, even more self-entitled fish from afar gather beneath you while you stand idly on the bridge, all of them begging... needing your attention.

The koi in this metaphor are your thoughts from the past. These fish will stay beneath you if you keep feeding them. I promise. So, too, will your thoughts continue to engage your computer brain if you feed them. The thoughts will stay there until you stop feeding them.

You are the one who controls whether you decide to feed the conversations in your brain. If you do engage with the anxious thoughts, then you feed your own thoughts and invite other thoughts to gather in your brain, one tangential thought at a time, just like the koi gathered.

Often, remind yourself that engaging or deliberating on any thought is exactly the reason you feel anxious with the chaos in your mind. Thoughts attract other thoughts. Thoughts do not help you arrive at peace. You will not sleep or relax while thinking good or frightening thoughts. Thoughts want to be fed, like the fish.

We cannot keep thoughts from popping in our head, just as we can't keep the fish from gathering beneath us. However, we can choose not to bring food to the bridge.

Tell yourself: When it's time to rest, no fish food!

None.

Chapter Four

The sun only reflects off the still waters. Be still!

CHAPTER FOUR:
Awake in the Brain;
Asleep in the Mind

In this chapter I will discuss some of the interesting ways your body and brain have learned to cope with life and how these coping skills interrupt your sanity. Remember, how you deal with your thoughts (for example: feeding them, dancing with them, and playing them over and over again in your brain) affect how you deal with anxious and fearful thoughts while you are awake.

There is a direct correlation between peace and how you deal with extraneous thinking. One often controls the other. For example, if you use some sort of smokescreen behavior to avoid anxious thinking, then peace will only happen during that habit. I have many clients who eat excessively, smoke, drink, get high, get angry, vape, even have sex to create a physical or metaphorical smokescreen around their anxiety.

The smokescreens, however, fade and the real problem returns with a hungry vengeance. You either continue feeding an addiction or you come to grips with the real problem, which hides beneath the smokescreen behavior.

More About Sensory Defensive People

If you feel as if you are especially sensitive all the time, certain physical things—especially irritants—will prevent a calm mind. This problem exists mostly for those of us who are classified as sensory defensive.

Sensory Defensiveness is a not-so-widely-known brain dysfunction that causes your neural pathways to fire faster than the average person. This causes normal sensory functions to feel amplified.

I remember the first time I realized that I was sensory defensive. I noticed how others handled pain so much more easily than I. A simple tap on the arm sometimes felt like a punch. A solemn gaze sometimes felt like a mean threat.

A sensory defensive person has neural pathways sending signals to and from her brain, then to all the different regions of her body at an extremely fast rate. Pain, movement, even stress can start with a big dose of fast neurotransmitters going to and from your brain. What starts out as a simple perfume as you enter a room or a reaction to a bright light through the windshield of your car may end up as a day-long migraine.

If I had a choice to look at this extra sensitivity and fast neural processing as empathic help from my angel guides or a curse from demons; I have to admit, at first, I felt as if it were a curse. Eventually, though, I realized I was simply different. These special sensitivities often protect me, too.

I hope that you will begin to see your sensitivities

as a benefit, rather than a hinderance. I will teach you to gain access to and control this sensory defensiveness with too much light, too much smell, too much noise, too much of just about everything, if you happen to fall within this spectrum.

Below is an important list that you should read closely. Be honest with yourself if:

- your senses are far more keen than those around you;
- you have been made fun of for being too sensitive;
- you are bothered by bright lights, loud noises, empathic feelings, such as the energies of other people in the room;
- if you think tastes and textures of food are intense;
- you can't tolerate certain smells (example: strong perfumes, intense cleaning liquids, or the detergent aisle at the supermarket); and
- you are extremely sensitive to hot and cold.

If you fall into *any* of these categories above, then you probably are somewhere on the spectrum of sensory defensiveness.

Don't be frightened about this diagnosis. Once you are aware of *Sensory Defensive* behavior, you can soon come to understand yourself in a way that you have never understood before.

As I said before, your author, is the poster child for this issue. A positive way forward exists for you as it did for me. I'm here to help. You may be comforted that I have been through many night terrors, childhood- and adult-PTSD, and have learned to manage all of this with great ease, as well.

From my earliest memories, my father, friends,

teachers, and my immediate family all said that I was too sensitive. In my early years I was known as Bobby. Bobby cried for many reasons, until he didn't. Then he held all his emotions closer than anyone knew.

A child should not hold his or her emotions inside if he or she wants to become a healthy adult. As a child, I found that when I expressed myself, organically, I became subject to even more ridicule. So, I just shut up and crammed my emotions into my body and heart.

I felt abnormal and wanted to be like everyone else in my family who was happy with dinner, slept throughout the night without nightmares, and didn't want to vomit at the sight of bologna, hot dogs, and mayonnaise.

If I shared with you how many times my four sisters tortured me with the food items I just mentioned, you would think they were sadists. They weren't. They were simply like everyone else in my life, insensitive to what it feels like to be acutely sensitive.

My late brother and father were the worst with their annoying comments about my sensory issues. I remember my father kicking me under the table at one restaurant, in particular, if I ordered something to my specifications and not to his.

My family used to go to a restaurant in rural Chippewa, Pennsylvania called the *19th Hole*. Obviously, it was near a golf course. It was famous for its fish sandwiches.

Only on a very special occasion, my father would treat the entire family to a fish sandwich, French fries, and a coke. Everybody's order sounded exactly the same. We were all expected, like child robots, to order what Dad brought us to this restaurant to eat.

However, when the waitress would come to me for my order, she asked as if she really wanted to know, "Okay, young man, what would you like?"

Then, I suddenly felt empowered to ask for what I really wanted. I asked for a toasted cheese, mashed potatoes, and an orange soda with no ice.

I didn't like the smell of fish. Mashed potatoes were fluffy like clouds. Ice made my teeth hurt. Yes, I was sensing far too many sensations for a seven-year-old child. (Even as an adult reading this, though, I think I would quite naturally want to slap that seven-year-old boy, if he were mine. Often, sensory defensive kids appear to the world as self-entitled brats.)

I was nothing near self-entitled nor a brat. In fact, I was *unentitled, disenfranchised, even.* All I wanted was to be normal.

My problems in restaurants amplified as an adult. My friends hated going out to dinner with me because of my pickiness. I can't tell you how many times my restaurant orders were wrong.

At one point in life, I thought the universe was simply laughing at me every time I ordered food in a restaurant. My orders never came back to the table with my carefully regarded specifications. I even would try to inject the word *please* two or three times while I ordered, specifying that I know my order is out of the realm of normal.

I would thank the server ahead of time for allowing me the grace to order with special requirements. Sometimes, I would even tell the waiter that I would be sure to tip accordingly for his or her kindness. I knew I was being picky. But, honestly, I would sit pouting and unable to eat if the food came out incorrectly.

Feeling too much of every emotion interfered with my life, my sleep, and my social interactions. The problems started at a very young age. I'm not sure when, but I thought everyone spent one to two hours falling asleep at night. Most scientific studies of adult sleep patterns show that a normal amount of time to fall asleep is thirty minutes.

I'd often wake up the next morning exhausted and unable to get ready for school with energy. I couldn't drink coffee because it made my stomach hurt. It wasn't until fifty was I able to drink one cup of decaffeinated coffee in the morning.

As a child, I couldn't share my difficulties with most people, because I'd get ridiculed. So, I was left with noone understanding my difficult childhood.

A couple of empathic teachers in high school seemed to understand that I was going through something traumatic. These beautiful angel teachers would often take me aside and treat me with a special word of advice or congratulations.

Besides being sensitive, my brain whirred like a computer as a teenager. As I said, sensory defensive people have neural pathways firing away like a machine gun on all levels. I was always thinking and always pondering situations as if something... anything... needed to be resolved. This made me a math and science whiz in high school.

Amazingly and seemingly from heaven, I did have a nice neighbor lady, Mary. She had no children of her own. When my mother left my father, Mary became my second mother. She would let me sit with her for hours. Most of the time, we were quiet. When I came home from school with my report card, I would run to her kitchen door, first. She was proud of me.

When I didn't have some game or gadget that the

other kids on the block owned, she and her husband Emil would make sure they bought me that gadget for my birthday or Christmas.

Getting to sleep at night often required me imagining what life would be like to be Mary's and Emil's child. As an adult, I still have dreams about being at their home.

Not everyone with adult sensory disorder has the same issues as I had. I'm telling you my story to prepare you for all that can affect adult sensory defensive behavior, especially anxiety, when your nervous system fires too quickly.

Trust me, my story has every one of the enumerated items that can cause anxiety and, ultimately, prevent peace or any kind of rest for the brain.

Perhaps, one of your children or a close friend seems to check off most symptoms on the list of issues facing adult sensory defensiveness. Maybe reading this will help enlighten that child or friend and help them, before anxiety becomes too caustic or painful.

Most sensitive children end up being acutely empathic as adults. Even at a young age, I could generally read people's intentions, feel their energy, or sense when something was wrong. I thought everyone had this power. I could also detect everything that was going on outside of me, including effects from a full moon, high tide, high- and low-pressure systems, rain, and storms.

Now, I'm almost as sensitive as a dog with smell. I can come into my home and, from the front door, immediately, detect a washcloth that is beginning to smell moldy in the bathroom in the farthest corner of the house, something most people couldn't even smell up close. I had to spend $900 on Dyson air purifiers for my home and office to get every smell out of the air, so that I wouldn't sniff around trying to find stinky culprits.

As I have said, this all sounds like it's a life that's too bright, too loud, too stinky, and too everything. However, I learned later in life that my sensitivity also gave way to my spiritual and empathic gifts as a human being. So, I'm okay with my differences, even delighted.

Getting to this self-acceptance took far too many years. I hope to help you or someone you know from the sadness I imposed upon myself for so many years, thinking I needed to be like everyone else to survive and be happy. In fact, I'm able to write this book because I have chosen to be empowered by my sensitivity.

I didn't learn how to turn off sensitivity and replace it with peace until way into my thirties. I did use my sensitivity to be distinctively on pitch in singing, cook with delightful herbs and spices, and was able to taste any entrée at a restaurant and figure out most of its ingredients before I was twenty.

As a musician, I have been a teacher who could listen to a student for one minute and figure out exactly what muscles he or she used that would hurt his or her voice. I also taught pitch-deficient clients, who most teachers found too difficult to guide.

Sensitivity to most things can help the sensory defensive person find his or her niche in life if one becomes aware of this pernicious default and recognizes it as a gift. One could be a wine taster, a chef, or an editor, because mistakes stick out like red flags on a white surface.

Sensory Defensive should be called Sensory Acute… or sensory aware… or sensory astounding.

One added note: All of my family, including my mom became sensory defensive in some way as they became older. Thanks to the grace of the universe that I found a husband who has SDD, as well. Together, we laugh at things that make us both nauseated that others are not bothered by.

We often take walks at night. We can smell everything in every home we pass, things that were eaten or smoked. We know if neighbors had been drinking alcohol, grilling out, or if their television or music is sounding too loud. We often wonder how the neighbors don't complain. Then we realize that the problem is not outside. The issue is within our own sensitive brains.

Mouth Agape

Not every anxious person has SDD. Some people have suffered some Post Traumatic Issue that has caused neural pathways that fire too quickly. This, of course, causes you to feel as if your heart is pounding from too much caffeine.

> *If you breathe with your mouth open,*
> *this also causes a fight, flight,*
> *or freeze response to the body,*
> *resulting in a rapid heart rate.*

Breathing with your mouth open contributes to receiving up to 20% less oxygen in the body. A Harvard study in 2020 shows that how you breathe (from the mouth or nose) can directly affect your health.

(https://www.health.harvard.edu/mind-and-mood/relaxation-techniques-breath-control-helps-quell-errant-stress-response)

People who snore or have untreated sleep apnea

are vulnerable to waking with high levels of fight, flight, or freeze hormones (extra cortisol, and adrenaline), produced by the adrenal glands of your sympathetic nervous system. An overabundance of these adrenal gland chemicals cause your body to want to escape danger. *Is it any wonder you feel awake and agitated all night, when you should be resting peacefully?*

Many people use medical tape to close and keep their mouths shut while they sleep. Even in my hypnosis practice, clients who tape their mouths shut at night seem to be alleviating a lot of night terrors and anxiety.

Don't Blame Yourself

The following explanation can tend to get a little complicated and wordy. Keep reading, though, as I explain things in simpler terms and with examples as we move forward.

The thinking and feeling receptors in the brain's cortex (the largest mass of the brain, the cognitive part) and deductive thinking are in direct opposition to relaxation. The *sympathetic* nervous system, which is meant to *activate* the fight, flight, or freeze part of the nervous system helps humans quickly get out of dangerous situations. However, the sympathetic nervous system also activates us for tasks and exercise.

HUMAN NERVOUS SYSTEM

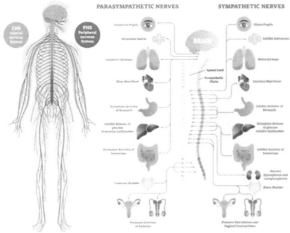

In anxiety patients, though, I notice that the sympathetic regions of the nervous system are also set off by a memory or even a nightmare.

So, why call this part of the nervous system *sympathetic*? At least, this is what I asked myself. Doesn't sympathy mean kindness and compassion?

The etymology of the word *sympathetic* means the connection between parts. In the 18th century, the scientist Jacob B. Winslow began to use this term relating to the nervous system, because of the codependent-dependent anatomy of the human nervous system.

For the sympathetic nervous system to work quickly and efficiently, without even the frontal lobes of the brain knowing or being cognizant of this lightning speed response of the amygdala, all the ganglia (these are synaptic relay stations between neurons on the spine) must work in tangent with each other—*in sympathy with each other*—for our fight, flight, or freeze system to work quickly and most efficiently.

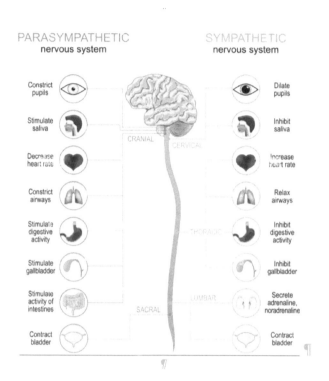

Professor Dave Explains:
https://www.youtube.com/watch?app=desktop&v=DPWE
hl7gbu4

On the other side of sympathetic nervous system is an even more confusing term. The *parasympathetic* part of the autonomic nervous system, which is the part of this interesting paradox that helps you relax and reach peace after a scary and fearful event. Parasympathetic sounds more like the opposite of sympathy.

For that reason, I want to clear this up. So, the opposite of the sympathetic nervous system is para-sympathetic, the part that relaxes you.

The reason why this part is called *parasympathetic* is because these relaxers work in coordination with the central nervous system by means of the *ganglion or synaptic relays*.

In other words, the parasympathetic nervous system lets the brain know it is out of danger and time to relax. Whereas the sympathetic system must work without informing the part of the brain that understands—to be most effective and the quickest in its response to danger.

For example: if your fight, flight, or freeze nervous system waited for you to know that you were in danger, it would be too late for any human in danger to respond. The person in the driver's seat of a car, for example, on his cellphone may not be paying enough attention to see a biker who came from a blind spot and was cruising toward him. If that driver thought about the biker, checked out what she looked like, observed her for even one second too long, it would be too late for the poor biker. The foot on the brake needs to operate faster than your understanding of the cyclist to be useful in this and other scary situations.

The sympathetic nervous system is designed to work on the quickest of impulses, so fast that the understanding part of the brain doesn't even know what happened until after the response occurs. The sympathetic nervous system saw the biker, even though the brain wasn't paying attention. The sympathetic responder acts like this ultra-sensitive, hyperaware, very cognizant angel driving along with you. Sometimes, we call this near-magical response, God.

After your amygdala helps you slam on the brakes and not kill a young woman riding a bike, you might say, "Thank God!"

This is important: If you are suffering or think you are suffering from PTSD or an anxiety disorder, you should know that the sympathetic nervous system can *push you* into fight, flight, or freeze, whether in the moment of danger, after the incident, or even in a *perceived situation of danger*. The sympathetic nervous system's response of a boatload of extra cortisol and epinephrine (another name for adrenaline) happens *without your understanding*.

Try to let that sink in! Reread it. It's important. PTSD happens without understanding or logic. It's an automatic response of your nervous system. So, stop thinking you can change something that is autonomic.

Your sweaty hands, palpitating heart, nauseous stomach, and muddled mind happen before you ever get the chance to tell yourself that you're not in danger. In fact, the sympathetic nervous system in the anxious man or woman is firing on all cylinders before the person can get the opportunity to realize what has happened.

This is important news for those suffering from anxiety and PTSD. They wonder why they are always so frightened and triggered for unknown reasons. Well, this part of the nervous system that determines your safety, the sympathetic nervous system, acts without your permission or your understanding.

If you don't understand the dynamics of the brain's workings, you'll blame yourself. You will misread your own thoughts and seemingly irrational reactions to those thoughts and nightmares. You will wonder why you can't control your anxious responses to what seems to be normal conditions, causing you even more anxiety. That's why you need special help to unlock the triggers to that nervous system and unhook from this bizarre response to a flashing light, a ceiling fan, or woman scolding her child.

You need to have this information about the sympathetic and parasympathetic nervous system's responses to keep the two ways the nervous system responds separate and to get on the correct side of a peaceful situation.

Anxiety in the Middle of the Night

Night terrors began happening to me in my early thirties. Late at night and before dawn, I would get dressed and run around the block a few times to become tired. Before sleep medications were available to me or before I knew they existed, if sleeping was impossible, I would drink alcohol to get tired and then blackout. I would only drink to fall asleep when my sleep problems were severe, which, in my case was when I spent three to four days without proper sleep.

When anyone is sleep deprived, he or she will, sometimes, do just about anything to get that much needed rest. Of course, I don't recommend drinking alcohol to blackout for any reason. But I'm sharing my past experiences to help you understand that an unruly mind causes anxious and extreme behavior.

Why, though, would you wake up to a rapid heart-rate after you had fallen asleep? This didn't make sense when it happened to me. The closest any kind of research had led me to was night terrors. This brings you to another one of your initial reasons for anxiety— fear of something that you don't understand. These moments feel as if they are ambiguous or generalized fear. The fear feels so far out of reach that you can't even imagine letting go of it.

I believe the reason I had awakened with terror and was filled with enough energy to escape a wildfire was that my subconscious never felt a reasonable amount of security—ever—not as a child and continuing into adulthood. When I would reach a deep sleep, sometimes, my subconscious would uncover something terrifying and wake me up with my heart racing.

The fight, flight, or freeze part of the brain, the amygdala, does not know the difference between reality and dreams. If you experience fear in the middle of the night, you may wake up with your heart beating and adrenalin pumping into your heart, making your body feel wired for a marathon.

Changing subconscious behavior took many years of therapy and hypnosis to see a minimal amount of positive effect. I had to uncover the ghosts that were literally still in my closet. As a gay man who had suffered sexual abuse as a child, going back into the closet to rescue my inner child was a place I was not willing to go for a long time. Too many ghosts. Too much terror.

However, now, even if a client is not ready to dig deeply for his or her hidden fears, I still can use hypnosis and the Zeroing-Out method to retrain the parasympathetic, autonomic nervous system, which activates to calm you. This part of the brain has memorized fight, flight, and freeze behavior from negative events in your past.

Because of the neuroplasticity of your brain, you are able to retrain these nervous system responses with time and diligence.

This was my -aha- moment.

Of course, I am barely touching the scientific surface of this research into your brain's responses to negative stimuli. For the purpose of this book, I'll not move any deeper than these important facts:

Review:
- The sympathetic nervous system triggers a fight, flight, or freeze response in the body with excessive amounts of adrenaline and cortisol. Adrenaline makes your heart beat much faster. Excess cortisol can make you stay on high alert and triggers the release of glucose (sugar) from your liver for fast energy during times of stress. When you don't need it, cortisol can make your mind feel muddled and keep your blood sugar levels high.
- The parasympathetic nervous system stops the flow of these chemicals and triggers calm.
- The sympathetic nervous system doesn't know the difference between perceived danger and actual danger.

We are fortunate the nervous system has neuroplasticity, allowing us to retrain what had been off-line and broken for so long. Neuroplasticity is the ability of neural networks in the brain to change through growth and reorganization. It is when the brain is rewired to function in some way that differs from how it previously functioned. Hypnosis, EMDR, and the Zeroing-Out Method retrain this part of the brain for peace.

CHAPTER FIVE:
The Opposite of Peace

After a traumatic event, we tend to carry some anxiety about any similar situation into the future. A small amount of this anxiety, however, can keep you on the verge of panic. If you have been diagnosed with posttraumatic stress disorder or PTSD, then you have a tragic or terrifying event that is anchored in your subconscious mind. Like a ferocious tiger crouching down, PTSD allows your brain to silently search for danger from anything that even looks like the original culprit. These signs may appear in dreams and when something similar appears when you are awake.

PTSD can also cause a low level of *daily* anxiety to sustain fear just enough that it creates an overage of cortisol and adrenaline, keeping you awake most of the night or feeling on the edge of panic. Most times the triggers are hidden from your understanding, awakened mind. Remember the allegory I shared in Chapter One about coming home to find a ferocious tiger lurking in your front yard.

Lurking Fear

My mother had had far too many surgeries for one woman. She was 88 when she began to show signs of *mental deterioration*. She was in pain most of the day. At night, she tended to remain awake, even though she was extremely tired. I believe that the reason she couldn't sleep was because she was afraid of not waking up at all.

It's difficult to talk to a parent with this kind of fear lingering in her brain. For three months she was bombarded with confusion and a lack of memory that kept her from knowing the difference between day and night. She had Sundown Syndrome, which means she got more confused in the evenings while trying to sleep and waking up frequently to use the bathroom because of diabetes.

When my mother was in my home visiting, I always made sure I had something planned for her the next day. I kept days regimented. We got up at a specific time together. We ate at a specific time. We went on a walk at a certain time.

This regimentation is so important when you get older and most importantly when your worst fear begins to awaken—fear of death.

Anxious people must plan what will occur directly after their perceived fear, especially if it's a known fear. For instance, if you're afraid of flying: while on the plane, imagine what you'll say to your family and friends as you meet them in the airport after the flight.

Fears can sometimes live inside you for much too long, growing like cancer. There is an old legend from the Middle Ages. A citizen was arrested by an angry Baron. He was taken down dark stairs—down, down,

down by a ferocious jailer who carried a great key a foot long and thrust him into a dark dungeon. The door shut with a bang.

The citizen lay in that dark dungeon for twenty years. Each day the jailer would come. The big door would open with a great creaking. A pitcher of water and a loaf of bread would be thrust in. Then, the door closed again.

After twenty years the prisoner decided that he could not stand this seclusion any longer. He wanted to die, but he did not want to commit suicide. So, he decided that the next day, when the jailer came, he would attack him. The jailer would then kill him in self-defense, and ultimately, the citizen's misery would end.

He decided to examine the door to be prepared for the next day when the jailer entered. To his amazement, the large door wasn't locked. Actually, there was not even a lock on the door. All those years he had not been locked in the dungeon—except in his mind.

At any time he could have opened the door, if only he had known... if only he had tried to escape his misery.

People usually don't become ready for big changes until they hear a deadly prognosis. Then they are somewhat forced to change. This happens because they are no longer able to do what they normally do in their life to make them happy. Life seems to push them on their way to change. Even still, they resist.

For example, with a fear of planes and flying, you may experience the need to change your irrational fear when you must fly to your daughter's wedding on another continent. When you must do something that grips you with that old fear, then you push at the fear strongly and make a shift in your thinking.

The other choice is that life goes on without you. This is the moment when most people choose a psychiatrist, a psychologist, a therapist, or a hypnotist. They are forced into a new behavior to make the much-needed change. Regular talk therapy and pills are often too slow for people who have an immediate desire for change.

Facing fear is much different than alleviating it. Having had PTSD for three things in my past, I have found that releasing it completely from the nervous system is virtually impossible. It would be like asking my mind and body to *completely* forget sexual abuse or someone dying in front of me. I don't believe this is possible.

I'm in my sixties and have tried every kind of nonmedical intervention to get rid of this subconscious crouching tiger, including standing in a below-zero Cryogenic tank for three minutes to reset my parasympathetic nervous system. Still, PTSD lurks far beneath the surface, perhaps, a little closer than before. Retraining the nervous system is slow. But with deep-seated PTSD and an anxiety disorder it is well worth your time to go through EMDR and hypnosis to help.

Trying to release PTSD is like telling a forensic computer technician that he can't find something that was on a cellphone or computer in the past. Of course, the technician can *and will* find any information that was once on any device.

Psychiatry believes that the tiny amygdala of the brain is responsible for sending PTSD fear responses from the nervous system before the deductive mind can recognize it. This means that no one can rationalize a PTSD fear. Not even the healthiest person on Earth can.

We simply don't have the time to rationalize PTSD

before the subconscious has already begun reacting. The amygdala sends a signal to emit fight, flight, or freeze chemicals in our body in less than a second, before the understanding part of our brain can reason.

How are you to teach yourself calming techniques, if your amygdala has already reacted before your understanding?

At this point, I probably don't need to convince you that Zeroing-Out and hypnosis therapies—to retrain the sympathetic nervous system—are what you need to convince the subconscious mind that you are safe from even the remnants and fragments of the trauma in your past.

Hypnosis gently invites you into the dream state and triggers the more essential parasympathetic nervous system to calm you in tense situations.

Zeroing-Out works in the cognitive brain to make room for peace. This is like carrying around an Epi-Pen in case of a heart attack. You'll want to use it when your brain gets cluttered, and you need to empty it like the cache on your computer, sometimes daily.

Eye Movement Desensitization and Reprocessing

There is another hypnotic technique called EMDR which works on retraining old patterns in the amygdala. This uses bilateral stimulation of the brain to unhook and unmemorized negative feelings and thoughts. Basically, the brain and eyes have a symbiotic connection. When your eyes move left, you use your left brain's hemisphere. When your eyes move right, you use your right brain. So, when you move your eyes back and forth, from left to right, this acts as an eraser.

With a good EMDR therapist, you can bring up old emotions and diminish their impact from using

EMDR therapy. This has worked with many of my clients suffering from anxiety. I use it in conjunction with and right before hypnosis. This seems to be the gold standard in my office.

Even sound therapy like Alpha Isochronic tones can be something that encourages the brain to release memorized fear responses. We need all of the above to help use the brain's neuroplasticity to create effective change.

In other words, we do have the ability to retrain those hyper neurotransmitters. The problem is that most people try to alleviate anxiety with one modality alone or talk therapy. If the amygdala triggers your sympathetic nervous system even while you sleep or with unknown triggers, how can talk therapy alone help?

We need to convince both the understanding brain and the subconscious that we are secure. For that, we need a full battalion of modalities.

Practice Makes Peace

The relaxation process is a practice. I'm still rehearsing after thirty some years of meditating and self-hypnosis. I liken this practice to a singer. I wake up with basically the same physical and musical instrument, the vocal chords, but with a different set of circumstances daily.

Some days my throat is dry. Sometimes it's sore. Some moments, before I sing, I'm frightened, and adrenaline keeps me from controlling my diaphragmatic breathing. There are numerous variables that can happen with a voice, the physical singing instrument.

Once, I had to sing with laryngitis, which seems impossible. But it wasn't. I've had to sing with the flu. I did this, as well. I've had to lower the key to a song to manage getting around having no high voice because of a cough or cold. The scenarios of a singer are varied and constantly changing.

The instrument itself, the larynx, is the same, but many things can affect how this instrument works on a daily and hourly basis. Very recently, I had spinal surgery on my third vertebra. The surgeon went in from the front of my neck and had to move my larynx to the side to replace the damaged vertebra, which houses the vocal cords. In the process my vocal cords were overstretched. What once was a larynx that worked to sing, has now become vocal chords that struggle even to talk. I'm told this will change in time.

The metaphor of a singer to his voice is the same as the metaphor for the body to the person working to relax. You wake up with the same body every day, but the circumstances and triggers are always changing.

Sleep can be simply sleep. But every time you get tired and go to your bed for rest, you have a different set of circumstances that change the process of sleeping. You are the same person, but everything going on in your life, and in your head, and every ache or itch in your body can change the process of sleep almost completely.

Will you ever find a complete answer for peace of mind? Well, without taking a prescriptive medicine that knocks you out, I guess the answer is no. You will always have to manage the changes and shifts in your life to create a new pathway to peace.

Is this discouraging for you? I certainly hope not.

This process is your bodily function and system to control. It's not mine or anyone else's body. It's yours.

So, if you want to create a healthier life for yourself, you must take each individual circumstance and adapt to it.

Let's face a reality right now:

Everything in your life changes, every day. Every part of your body ages, every second of every day. We are all on the way toward the demise of our physical body—death. This is fact.

Getting comfortable with this fact and even seeing yourself gracefully accepting this fact is inevitable and quite necessary to live a life rich in the present moment. Adapting to this process is the only way forward without fear.

As you try to relax, there may be certain circumstances that could cause you to deal with something outside of your control, such as pain in your physical body, trouble breathing because of a stuffy nose, or even snoring issues (your problem or that of your sleep partner). These are sensory complications that could cause a varying set of acute awareness issues.

For instance, you may be falling asleep as it begins to thunder and rain outside. A storm may cause some people to fall asleep. But, my dog stayed up all night quivering in the bathtub. I could hear his tiny toenails clinking on the porcelain tub.

The rain is calming to me. However, a clap of thunder feels like someone is standing behind a corner and leaping out in front of me, intending to *scare the crap out of me.*

My husband often stands behind something and tries to scare me. When my heart stops for a second, and I scream like a little girl, he thinks it's funny. As I get older and realize my physical body is a carbon copy of my ancestry, the likelihood of me having heart problems is high.

You could be dealing with back, hip, or foot pain. I have many clients who complain that as soon as they get to a sleepy place, they have neuropathic pain shoot to their hands and feet. How could anyone possibly relax with such a problem?

However, you must always consider everything going on in your life as just a minor setback. If you need to seek help for someone to ferret out what needs to be changed in your behavior, then do it! No amount of money can take the place of a life without stress or a great night's sleep.

Situations change. New drugs get discovered every day. People like me and you with these problems are setting out daily to overcome holistically and sometimes without drugs. You are definitely not the only one experiencing any one particular situation. In fact, check out these facts from sleepfoundation.org:

- 264 million people worldwide suffer from anxiety;
- Between 10% and 30% of adults struggle with chronic insomnia;
- It is believed that between 30% and 48% of older adults suffer from insomnia;
- People with generalized anxiety disorder (GAD) experience restlessness, irritability, difficulty concentrating, chronic fatigue, nausea, dizziness, and worsening worry or fear over extended periods of time;
- Women have a lifetime risk of insomnia that is as much as 40% higher than that of men;
- As many as 15-30% of males and 10-30% of females meet a broad definition of obstructive sleep apnea (OSA); and
- GAD affects 6.8 million adults in the United States, and women are twice as likely to be affected as men.

You and I are not suffering alone. I hope this makes you feel better. It makes me feel better that I'm not the only one in the world who has had to overcome obstacles. At this very moment, I feel that I'm a part of a big tribe of distinctive, yet unusual, individuals who thrive during, and through, abject adversity.

I hate that people are suffering needlessly, though, especially when I know I can help some of their problems. I'd like to think that I help everyone who comes into my office, but the actuality of that idea is probably not possible.

For example, I have had a client come to my office to release the idea that her husband thinks her symptoms of pain are fabricated. So, if she were to leave my office with an answer or a resolution to her pain, then her husband would be correct. He said, *"It was all in her mind."*

So, leaving my office *healed* is not actually something she wanted to happen—not consciously or subconsciously. People, in general, want to be right, especially about the symptoms of their own bodies and minds.

As I said before, smoking cigarettes or pot is a literal and figurative smokescreen. Yet, people who come into my office to quit smoking have often convinced themselves that nothing will help them quit. They probably have even tried hypnosis before to stop but are willing to try again. Really? Have you ever tried to convince someone that quitting is possible when they have convinced themselves they will always have a habit? It's virtually impossible.

Many people fight the healing process. They are used to dealing with struggle every day of their lives. What would be the difference if they woke up and things changed for the better? What would they worry about? Could they get through the day without nervous acts of worry, controlling others, and caring too much about what others think?

Would you say *yes* to the secret to a perfect night's sleep or a sure way of alleviating your anxiety and stress?

When I discovered how to get to sleep, I was elated—so much so that I would test it over and over again. I can even fall asleep on a plane or in a room full of talking people. Nothing stops me from sleeping now. I have learned to take control of my situation and current circumstance.

Peace is no longer an illusion. Peace comes from taking what life hands you. You will sort through it. You will keep your well-learned lessons and throw out the junk that you don't need. Anxiety is simply junk. Let's change the way you act as a result of it—together.

Remember that the doorway to peace and happiness opens inward, just as the windows of your soul open inward.

Let's get rid of anxiety now with the Zeroing-Out Technique!

Zeroing Out

CHAPTER SIX:
Zeroing-Out: Stop the Story

To create good mental health, your first job is to get rid of the real problem—extraneous thinking or rumination.

A normal person uses the deductive brain at work and at school. Memorized facts make up the majority of our brain's usage. To arrive at rest and peace, however, we must take time to put aside what's rational. Put the deductive and memorized thoughts from the past in a metaphoric briefcase and lock it when the workday is over.

If you don't stop deductive thinking, then you will enter into meaningless conversations at home and with loved ones.

For example, you may find that financial worries are constantly looping on a metaphoric merry-go-round in your brain. Then, a loved one initiates a meaningful conversation with you. However, your mind is still affixed on work, so you give that person a modicum of your attention; certainly, not what they deserve. You simply cannot focus on work thoughts and normal conversations with friends and family. This is an impossibility. Without releasing work thoughts and memories from the past, peace is also not possible.

The Blank Brain: Zeroing-Out

Yesterday, after 45 days with no simple carbs, I was driving by a donut shop. I thought that my brain had taken over my legs and arms, with my trigger foot on the gas pedal, hands on the steering wheel, and my body with the urge to eat something sugary. I felt like a force inside of me led my car to the parking lot of Dunkin'.

Sitting in my car, I did these simple actions below. My cravings immediately went away. I use this series of actions with my clients who are working on irradicating an addiction like cigarette smoking or overeating. However, since physical habits are often mental habits, anxiety can be remediated in the exact same way.

You, too, can learn these basic steps. First, I'll teach you the simple Zeroing-Out steps. After, I'll describe in detail with photos exactly how to get to peace when you are stuck in your brain.

In full transparency, I received this series in a meditation. I can certainly conceive of the science behind this cognitive exercise, but science is not how this practice came to be. Just to let you know, this is something you probably will not find in any other book or find any hypnotists using, unless they have read this book or have been led by the same shining star.

Remember: There are two exercises below—the

first is shorter than the longer, complete exercise. I recommend that you learn the shorter one, first.

Then, after a week of using the shorter one, move on to the more complex exercise, which includes tapping, visualizing, and affirmations.

The Short Zeroing-Out Exercise

First memorize the following numbers in order: one, two, five, three, four, zero. Then, use your fingers to make the numbers without speaking them aloud. Try to memorize the hand movements without saying the numbers in your mind.

Then, do the following actions:

1. With your dominant hand, put up your forefinger in front of your face, palm facing you. (Use the same hand throughout the exercise and start each action with your eyes shut.)

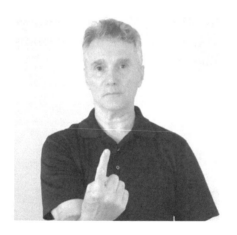

    Open and close your eyes, as if you are taking a mental snapshot of your finger, using your eyelids as a camera. (If you're old enough, you'll remember the old shutters in cameras that snapped open and closed when you took a photo. This is the same principle.)

2. Now put up two fingers. Open and close your eyes, as if you are taking a mental snapshot of your two fingers.

3. Switch to five fingers. Open and close your eyes, as if you are taking a mental snapshot of your five fingers.

4. Put up three fingers. Open and close your eyes, as if you are taking a mental snapshot of your three fingers.

Put up four fingers. Open and close your eyes, as if you are taking a mental snapshot of your four fingers.

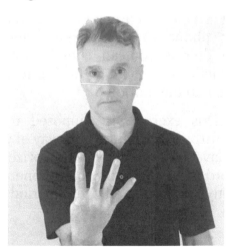

5. Lastly, make a fist. Instead of opening and closing your eyes, open them and say the word POWER as you look at Zero!

After you have memorized the sequence of fingers and fist, you can continue with the exercise below. I recommend using a voice recorder or voice memo function on your phone to record the following instructions. If you do this, you can listen to yourself speaking the instructions, instead of having to read them, first, and then do the motions.

Remember: This exercise is supposed to be confusing, so it disturbs every neural pathway of your brain. You don't have to immediately memorize the process if you record these words on your phone. You can listen and gently teach yourself over a period of a week.

Making This Process Easier. In the last chapter of the book, you will find private links to each of these processes on YouTube. If you watch the Zeroing-Out Techniques a few times, I assure you it will become easy for you. While you are at my YouTube Channel, go to my De-Stress videos for helpful hints about stress.

LONG ZEROING-OUT EXERCISE

The Zeroing-Out process includes EFT, aspects of EMDR, affirmations, and a complex cognitive mind memorization. All of these together are what cause the Zeroing-Out effect.

Clinical EFT (Emotional Freedom Techniques) is an evidence-based method that combines acupressure with elements drawn from cognitive and exposure therapies. The approach has been validated in more than 100 clinical trials. Its efficacy for PTSD has been investigated in a variety of demographic groups including war veterans, victims of sexual violence, the spouses of PTSD sufferers, motor accident survivors, prisoners, hospital patients, adolescents, and survivors of natural and human-caused disasters. Meta-analyses of EFT for anxiety, depression, and PTSD indicate treatment effects that exceed those of both psychopharmacology and conventional psychotherapy.

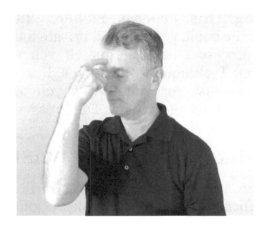

1. Begin with your eyes closed, as the majority of the exercise is done with your eyes shut, which is why I recommend recording the exercise or using the video links at the end of the book.

   With your dominant hand, put up your forefinger in front of your face, palm facing you. Use this finger to tap between your eyes in the area of the pineal gland or just between your eyes at your forehead.

   Tap there continually, while you say to yourself: "I'm going to begin a new thinking process!" Say this three times. Don't be afraid to tap hard. It's bone. It should sound hollow in your mind when you tap.

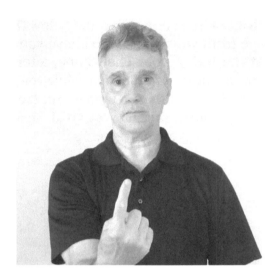

Now, put that same finger in front of your face. Open and close your eyes, as if you are taking a mental snapshot of your finger, using your eyelids as a camera. The movement should be eyes closed, open, closed.

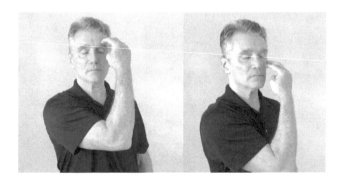

2. With eyes closed, switch your dominate hand to two fingers. Use these two fingers to tap twice on the bone above and below the opposite eye from your hand. Tap above your brow and at the top of your cheekbone, alternately and continuously.In your mind, while you tap, think of something you want to change. See the change, not the problem. Imagine a vivid image of you overcoming your problem.

Put your hand in front of your face and take a mental snapshot of your two fingers.

3. Switch your hand to five fingers now. Use all of your fingers and thumb to tap the top of your shoulder bone, including your clavicle. Use the shoulder opposite of your dominant hand to get the ultimate bilateral stimulation. (Notice we always tap bone.)

    While tapping, think of a person in your life that has your back and is encouraging. Imagine that person tapping your shoulder and saying the words, "You got this!"

    Put your hand in front of your face and take a mental snapshot of your five fingers.

4. Switch to three fingers. Use these fingers to tap below your bottom lip at your chin bone.

Make a commitment to yourself to always speak positively about the issues you face. For example: instead of: "I have a problem with food," say: "I am doing my best to eat healthy food."

Put your hand in front of your face and take a mental snapshot of your three fingers.

5. Now, switch your hand to four fingers. Karate chop the side of one hand with the opposite side of your other hand, like you're chopping away at something negative.

Think of a negative habit you want to release and change. Imagine chopping away at the problem until it's gone from your mind.

Put your hand in front of your face and take a mental snapshot of your four fingers.

6. Switch your hand to a fist (zero fingers). Use your fist to softly rub your heart in a clockwise circle with your palm facing your heart or tap gently on your chest in the heart area.

Think this: *I will make the next loving choice for myself.* Or you can make it more personal to your beliefs: *I can do all things with Spirit or God or Christ which strengthens me.*

7. Now take your fist in front of your face, open your eyes, and look at it. Keeping your eyes open, say aloud: "Power!"

CHAPTER SEVEN:
Adding Zeroing-Out to Your Life

The implementation of this exercise has provided an amazing way to add intention and tapping to the Zeroing-Out treatment. You can also use this exercise for a habit, physical pain, and emotional distress. The longer version is definitely the complete package for Zeroing-Out.

If you are in a place where you don't want people to notice you doing these complex actions, you can do this exercise silently, in your mind, without moving, tapping, or blinking. You simply imagine the entire exercise. It works just as well in the imagination, preferably with your eyes closed.

I do this in my mind, without the hand movements, after I close my eyes for sleep. Also, if I find that my mind isn't cooperating, I repeat the exercise over and over again, until my mind gets annoyed with me.

Anxiety sometimes acts like a disrespectful child. When you gain control over your unwieldy brain, you will know you are gaining control over the anxiety.

Using Zeroing-Out to Fall Asleep

I have a friend who tells me she is awake most of the night. She can tell me exactly what she thought during the night with perfect accuracy. When I told her about the idea of taking control of the deductive, thinking brain, she told me that she was willing to try my technique. She was immediately successful. Diligence is key here. The people who practice more often have the most success.

I watch clients fall into a light sleep almost every day in hypnosis sessions. In my personal life, I have had five brothers and sisters growing up and have had a few partners throughout my life, as many do. So, I've witnessed many people fall asleep.

To my great amazement, the people I slept with or watched usually fell asleep immediately, some even with their arms wrapped around me.

What did I feel? I experienced being trapped like a mouse in a trap. Drawn there with rich emotion and love, I was there willingly. I felt as if I couldn't breathe, though. The more they snoozed, the less I slept. Finally, I would gently break away from the embrace.

Most of the time, I would go to the couch, sit up, and try to fall asleep by myself, partially reclined. Sitting in a recliner has been a lifesaver before Zeroing-Out.

When your head is on the same level as your heart as with lying in bed, it is more difficult for sensory defensive people to fall asleep. A recliner provides a way for the head to be above the heart, which makes falling asleep easier.

I still use the recliner to nap. I often go to the recliner if I awaken in the middle of the night, as well. I enjoy the stillness I receive from falling asleep in a chair, on my back, and leaving my body completely in the warm embrace of the comfortable chair. Maybe, I should have married a chair.

For Sensitivity Before Falling Asleep

The concept of being partially reclined to fall asleep is something you can use if you have had insomnia in the past or have it currently.

1. Make up an extra bed at night on a recliner;
2. Falling asleep with your head above your heart makes your heart work a bit harder, causing you to fall asleep more quickly;
3. Sleeping with your head on the same level as the heart, for a sensory defensive person, will make you hear your own heartbeat and cause it to beat faster;
4. A weighted blanket on your body can confuse your neural pathways, as well. The weight does the opposite of exciting you; the weight then works with your parasympathetic nervous system to relax you, diverting your senses to the weight, like a baby would feel after swaddling; and
5. Ruminating or thinking deductive thoughts will prevent you from sleep every time.

One last note: In sleep studies, most people take 20-30 minutes to fall completely asleep. Use a very dark room or an eye mask to make your brain and body think that it is night for at least 30 minutes before you retire. Sleeping in front of a television, phone, or computer is not conducive for rest, because of the light.

Extra Steps for the Sensory Defensive

Always close your eyelids gently, not tightly. Make sure they are open just a small bit, enough to see a bit of light, but not enough to see an object. Your eye muscles may flutter a bit. This is a natural reaction.

Now, avert your eyes upwards, as if you are staring out the top of your forehead.

Try to imagine listening to, but not paying attention to your thoughts. I likened this theory to having a toddler who just learned to ask questions. After listening to incessant questions about everything, like: "Mommy why does this go boom?" "Daddy, why is your shirt blue and mine is white?" "Why is an apple red?" your patience begins to wear down and you begin to half listen.

This same listening skill is the feeling you want to give to those random thoughts floating through your physical brain. Listen to them, but don't pay attention to them enough to be bothered by them.

I don't believe in trying to fight thoughts. Fighting anything will only cause you to think more contradicting thoughts.

Rise above your human thoughts by focusing on the spiritual plane or the unseen truths and laws of the universe that present endless possibility.

Also, you can focus on listening for an answer to any question. After you ask a question to anyone, even God, you tend to stay quiet in the brain while waiting for the answer.

In your silence, try these questions:

- What do I need to focus on now?
- What is my next loving choice?

Be amazed at the capacity of understanding and fantasy you have. Feel a sense of awe at everything you know and see in your mind. This is the way that the mind supersedes the computer brain. Again, the doorway to the mind opens inward.

The chatter or chaos never stops in the human brain. We must rise so far above that chatter that we no longer hear it. It becomes a whisper, soft enough to lull you to sleep.

Sometimes, before I shut my eyes, I tell myself: I'm tired of thinking now. It's time to rest from the chaos of my thoughts.

Speaking to yourself with demands is much like self-hypnosis. It works. You are not crazy. Most people talk to themselves all day.

Very few people say to themselves: "If I'm talking, then who is listening?"

Zeroing Out

CHAPTER EIGHT:
Why Hypnosis?

In this chapter I will explain each portion of a hypnosis session to help you understand the mechanics of relaxing the body and the mind. To be successful, you should have an understanding of how the parasympathetic nervous system works (from Chapter One). The preparation for hypnosis, the breath work, the movement of the eyes, and the relaxation process is what a body needs to relax, meditate, or sleep.

I will give a detailed explanation of what I do to help someone retreat from an anxious mind. There are five sections. You will be able to understand why each step is necessary to move toward a meditative mind, or in some cases, sleep.

I believe in being goal oriented. Your job for the remainder of this chapter is simply to be an observer of the hypnosis process, which I detail next.

If you decide to make hypnosis your next loving

choice, this will help you to be prepared. Hypno-therapy, guided meditations, and progressive relaxation are very similar practices, requiring dedication to the process and the retreat from the sympathetic nervous system and the deductive brain.

A Question to Ask Yourself

First, this is the answer to the question that I want you to ask yourself. Memorize it, so that when you ask yourself the following question, there will be only one answer:

The Answer is: There is only one goal: peace of mind.

The Question: What is the only thing that is important right now?

Before you begin the process of erasure and hypnosis, there is only one important goal: to release the physical brain and body to make room for insight, creativity, and peace.

The Preliminary Exercise:

I prefer a recliner for hypnosis. If you use a bed, prop up your back and head with pillows.

Begin with your eyes open. Move your eyes upward toward the ceiling and inhale for five or six seconds, think about gathering light, peace, and healing from wherever you imagine those powers exist—in heaven, on Earth, within you, or in nature.

As you exhale, move your eyes toward your toes, using the exhale to let go of negativity. See the negativity going out of the bottom of your feet.

Use five seconds to inhale and exhale without any space between the inhales and exhales. When you elongate and balance the inhales with the exhales, you:

- Slow down your heart rate; and
- Lower your blood pressure.

Do this sequence with the breath and eye movement ten times.

If you are already relaxed, you may not need to work as hard to get your heart rate and blood pressure under control.

Before you begin the five steps to relaxation, below, ask yourself: *What is the only thing that is important right now?*

See if you can remember the answer.

Step #1: Positioning the Eyeballs and Eyelids

Gently close your eyes. With your eyelids closed, raise your eyeballs up and down, side to side, noticing what color, if any, that you see. This is an exercise for the mind. The color you see is what we will refer to as the **canvas of your mind**.

You'll notice that when you close your eyes, the color of the canvas doesn't change with the movement of the eyeballs.

The open eyes are connected to the deductive and inductive patterns of the brain. The closed eyes are connected to the mind or your creative source. What you see with closed eyes (no matter the color: black, grey, orange, white, multiple colors...) is what you see with your mind, using your imagination.

On the canvas of your mind create a circle the size of a cruise ship window. Notice you can see outside the window.

Keeping your eyes closed, just imagine staring up at the circle in your mind. Know that this circle is a doorway to another dimension outside of the canvas of your mind. The window can have a beautiful butterfly beckoning you to fly outside the window.

Carefully notice every color of the rainbow in the butterfly's body. Also, decide that the window is a doorway from your thinking, deductive brain to your dreaming mind.

Begin to intensify your internal gaze through this window onto the canvas of your mind's imagination, as if you are trying to discover what is on the other side of the window.

You should feel that your pupils are dilating or the muscles in the back of your eyes are relaxing and expanding.

Now, check to see if your eyelids feel locked. Don't try to force them open! Simple try gently to open them. If they do feel locked, you can move on to the next step.

You need to accomplish the locking of the eyelids before the next step. Practice until this method or the alternative method below works. One of these methods will work. I've never had anyone not be able to do one or the other of these exercises.

An Alternative Method

The following method is a more traditional hypnotic approach. It's called a walk-down, using the connection of your open eyes to the brain.

While in the reclined position, begin by staring up at the ceiling—at any point. Staring at one point slows down the brain.

Count backward slowly from 20 to 1. When you get to one, gently close your eyes with your eyeballs still pointed upwards at that point. Don't lose focus, even though you gently closed your eyes.

Again you will want to feel your eyelids are closed and locked.

Up to this point in the book, the inductive and deductive ways of thinking are the two processes of the brain. However, when we let go of the brain and its processing, what happens is that the mind gets liberated from the body completely. Like in sleep, you dream, usually without consciousness. This is the liberated mind.

The liberated mind has no limitation, I see it, rather, as the awakened imagination of possibility.

The bliss you will feel while meditating and in a successful hypnosis session is when you experience the weightlessness of the body and then the mind, which ushers you to the dream state.

Without keeping some part of the brain awake, there would be no chance that your human self could physically and mentally experience this existential peace. Distinguish the difference!

What Is the Mind?

Your mind is not your computer brain. The mind is the place where your dreams, your intuition, and creative images exist.

As you peer into the darkness, beneath your eyelids, you use your mind only.

Continue to look through the lens of your mind onto the canvas and through an imaginary window while you begin the first breathing exercise.

Yogis have been using this partially awake, mostly-asleep phenomenon for centuries. The *asana*, or movement practice in yoga is to lead your fatigued body to total relaxation while you still remain conscious enough to experience the release. The practice of *shavasana*, or corpse pose, at the end of the of yoga class is designed to let go of the physical body and become aware of only the breath, the *prana*.

Step #2: Accessing the Observer Mind

Try to imagine that you are floating near a round window on the ceiling. Pretend you can observe your own physical body beneath you. It's as if your mind, the part of you that is watching from above now holds a remote control for all your body parts, your mind, and even your breath control.

Imagine this Observer uses the remote control to turn off parts of your body, starting from your feet and going upwards to your head.

If you notice that any muscle in your body is particularly tight, with the *remote control of your mind*, tighten that muscle a little, hold that muscle for three seconds, then release it. This should take care of releasing any muscle tension in the physical body.

After you finish shutting down the physical body, one limb at a time, take another sweeping look from the Observer part of the mind to see if any residual tension exists in the physical body. To rest completely you must get the muscles in your physical body to feel completely free of tension.

The longer your body stays motionless, the more weightless you will feel. Objectively, you want to feel as if the entire body is no longer being controlled by the brain and is completely still with no movement. When parts of the body are relaxed enough, they begin to feel numb.

A hypnotist may say to you, "You could move your legs if you wanted to, but they are so relaxed that it's difficult to imagine moving them. In fact, you can't move them at all. It feels magical and light for your legs to be released from your brain.

"Your arms, hands, and feet, also, feel completely released from your control. Your body feels light. You could float right off the recliner."

When you have accomplished this release, on your final controlled breath, feel as if you are releasing your Spirit or your consciousness from your physical body through the portal above you and behind you. Let your spirit fly freely without the body.

Observe your body but let it rest completely. Your body and mind deserve to rest.

Step #3: Release the Control of the Breath

You are not giving away control of any part of you in this portion of the exercise. You are *providing a way* to the Observer Mind.

To accomplish this, you must imagine your consciousness is outside your body. Feel your breath happening *to* you. Let your body breathe you.

Leading the body and mind through its natural stages of release, you may experience quick breaths, at first. Others may feel that the body is completely still for a long time, before it needs its next breath.

Nothing you feel or experience is bad or wrong. It's important to remember not to judge what happens during this process. Just observe your humanness and take your time to let go of it.

If it helps, imagine that you have angels or positive spiritual influences all around you. The angels will take care of your human body while you leave it for your journey into the dream state of your mind. We don't need the physical body or brain to experience the next phase of this exercise.

Step #4: Don't Let the Natural Impulses of the Body Interrupt Your Rest

As you pull away from the control of the body, realize that the body doesn't need to move or itch itself or reposition itself. You don't need to move, because you are imagining what the body would be like during sleep. It doesn't need your attention while you sleep. You don't even need to respond to a sudden itch, a cough, or a random movement. Just observe the body and its issues. Let the body act organically, as if it were asleep.

Brain Resistance

You may notice that the computer brain doesn't want to be left alone or dismissed. If the voice of the computer brain is not heard, it thinks it will die. So, it will struggle to gain your attention.

You may cough or choke and wonder if you need some water. You may do these things... but remember, the brain is really trying hard to keep you awake and anxious. That's its job. However, you really want to find the path to the creative, Observer Mind, so you may listen and comfort your body, but appease it and nothing more.

Recognize that your body is acting more like the little child who doesn't want to go to bed. Don't be the parent trying too hard to comfort him at your own expense. Recognize the petulant child is manipulating you. So, you shut off the light and say, "Okay, now, Daddy has to go to sleep. So, if you call me again, I may not hear you."

You must teach your body to trust your mind. It deserves your trust. The mind is the strongest and most important part of your thinking function as a human.

A petulant child needs your attention and your care, but he or she doesn't need you to intercede or scold it every time he or she acts up. If you were to do that to a child, the child would get the impression that she *had to act up* to get your attention.

So, too, with the body. The body is like your own child at this point of the learning process. Coddle it, but also be stern, so you will not indulge it and teach it bad habits. You have already put your child to bed (your body). With certainty, you don't need any water. You don't need to go to the bathroom. You don't need food.

The child is ready for bed, even though he or she wants your attention and may even cry and tug at your heartstrings. With love, you carefully remove yourself from the child's room, perhaps leaving a light on or a stuffed animal beside him to help him feel safer.

A careful balance exists here between the crying child and the all-knowing parent. Learning to fall asleep is about finding this balance between parenting and gently resisting the need to coddle the crying baby within. Even a parent will sometimes wait outside the child's room and be sure she is okay. This is your job, too. However, you can do this by simply observing.

You have heard horror stories about babies with all-night tantrums. Perhaps, they had never been taught to be alone. Being alone and feeling safe is a learned behavior.

When a parent returns to the room when he or she is truly needed, the baby begins to understand that love returns, and it doesn't need to behave poorly for attention.

This metaphor is so important. With absolute certainty you will return to your body's needs when you're ready to feed it or do whatever it needs to be comfortable the next morning.

Your awakened brain with deductive thoughts is not an abandoned child. You are a trusting child with a great parent who returns when the child is truly in need.

After you successfully leave autonomous control to your body, you feel liberated emotionally, physically, and spiritually—be still. This is a peculiar paradigm, though, because you can now feel as if your mind is like the remote control center of your body. You could control it from outside yourself, *if you wanted,* however, you do not want to control it. You set the remote control down.

You are not trapped in this position. You want to be here, so it's easy to let go to these annoying awakened brain sensations.

One caveat: If you do have a persistent cough, tell yourself that once the coughing stops, you will very easily return to your quiet space. "Coughing or sneezing will not prevent you from total rest." I have plenty of clients who are trying to quit smoking and have *smoker's cough.* I suggest to them that they may cough throughout the night, but they sleep despite of the cough. This is the same circumstance.

This liberated place outside of the body is now free from the physical attention of the awakened brain. You will get excellent and perpetual love while sleeping and all the mental rest that meditation affords you.

If you feel something different than peace in this place outside of the body, start over or get professional hypnosis.

When You Get Lost in a Thought

If you get stuck, feel trapped, or find yourself in an old thought, just start back at the beginning and make another attempt at finding that exit from your thoughts. You may need to experience this new pathway many times before you memorize the direction to your destiny. Relaxation is a learned behavior, as is meditation.

Don't be annoyed with trying. This is a process, a practice. Eventually, you won't need to practice as often to get to peace. However, be like the athlete in training. Do this as many times as you need to be a success.

Without beating yourself up with thoughts of never being able to achieve this result, simply begin again. Trust that the peace for which you search exists outside of your deductive, computer brain. This is the main goal. Don't pay attention to any voice in your brain that tells you otherwise.

The sleeping mind speaks in images, not voices in your head. It's easy to distinguish a voice from an image.

So, you can release the voices of chaos for now and simply search with your inner eyes for the peace you deserve and require.

Step #5: Invite Your Imagination to Dream

Remember how the actor trains to say his lines with depth and meaning? Sometimes we need a *mental equivalent* to provide a clear emotional memory to help us along to an authentic feeling.

A mental equivalent is an added feeling to your imagination to encourage your mind to move beyond simple dreams to experiential ones.

For example: I may want to imagine prosperity. I would see my bank account with a million dollars in it. If I hadn't ever had a million dollars, then I would imagine a mental equivalent that felt like I had a million dollars, such as a moment in time when my life felt abundant and overflowing with spiritual riches, instead of physical ones.

Up to this point, your mind has been controlling the latter part of this process. Now it's time to let go even of your mind.

You don't need to blink, because your eyes are

closed, so just stare with your mind's eyes. You don't need to simply look forward either. The space within your mind has no physical eyes. You can see in all directions. Stare as if you are surrounded by benevolent love.

Let dreams happen. You can *invite* dreams by letting go, but you can't *make* them happen.

> *You can't make a dream. Dreams come to you. They float up from your subconscious mind. Give them silence and space.*

Let your silent gaze reveal your dream's destiny. You are totally letting go to whatever peace and assurance this moment has for you. It's safe and perfect.

Receiving Your Free Hypnosis Recording

You may be saying to yourself, just about now: "I'll never be able to remember all of this."

Never fear. You may request a private link to my two videos demonstrating the short and long Zeroing-Out processes.

Go to my website and follow the directions below: https://www.bosebastian.com.

Look around the website. Go to the page, "Need to Know." Near the bottom you will find links to Bo's Blog. There you will find many helpful articles, including many about sleep, anxiety, and interesting life issues.

Shop around in the "Store" section, as well, where you'll find my twelve other books and the links to purchase them.

If you have any interest in my speaking series, you

can go to the Seminars Link.

To receive the free hypnosis video links, you must follow these instructions below:

After going to the website, at the bottom of the "Need to Know" page, you will find "Contact Us." Click the "Call or Text Now" button. You won't actually call me. This goes directly to a page that texts or emails me a message indicating that you contacted me. Simply add the message: **"Send me your Video Tape Links for Zeroing Out."**

Make sure you type in your email correctly, so that I can respond accordingly. Periodically, you may get a message about a new book or a place where I'm speaking. If you don't want that to happen, you can just unsubscribe at any time.

Also, please share any great thoughts about the book you enjoyed or didn't understand. Great 5* Amazon Reviews are always helpful in spreading the word.

THE END

ABOUT THE AUTHOR

Bo Sebastian is a clinical hypnotherapist and owner of Hypnosis on Las Olas in South Florida. He has a De-Stress channel on YouTube and is active on most social media. Bo has written 12 books, any of which can be found on Amazon.com or your local- or online bookstore. Bo is married and lives in South Florida. He often speaks around the country, helping people with anxiety and stress.

Made in United States
Troutdale, OR
04/20/2025

30756763R00076